Dear
John & Jill
Enjoy !
Love.
Ed + Arlene

dirt
is good
for you

dirt
is good
for you

True Stories of Surviving Parenthood

by the editors of Babble.com

CHRONICLE BOOKS

SAN FRANCISCO

Library of Congress Cataloging-in-Publication Data available.

ISBN 978-0-8118-7118-1

Design by Jennifer Tolo Pierce.

Manufactured in Canada.

10 9 8 7 6 5 4 3 2 1

Chronicle Books
680 Second Street
San Francisco, California 94107

www.chroniclebooks.com

 babble

contents

foreword

We created Babble.com for one very simple reason: we couldn't
find a magazine or community that spoke to us as new parents.
Every publication we encountered presented procreation as a cute
and cuddly experience, all pink and powder blue, at best an interior
decorating opportunity, at worst a housekeeping challenge. Please.
None of it was true to the experience we were having, and that we
saw around us.

The truth is that parenting is one of life's crucible experiences—
it's rapturous, backbreaking and hysterically funny. It swiftly cures
both diehard cynics and careless naifs. It's a primal, somatic journey,
thick with the fragrances, stenches, coos, and cries of life at its most
elemental. It's a subject, in other words, that deserves both serious
and lighthearted attention from the great writers of our day.

This, then, is part of Babble's mission: to tell the truth about
parenting, to bypass the clichés and dig into the magical and maddening reality. We wanted to explore the world of parenting on a
daily basis with ruthless honesty, and with the humor and lyricism
natural to the subject.

We can't think of a more interesting time to be talking about
parenting. A few decades ago, things were simpler—parents followed

uncontested instructions from the family doctor; wives did most of the work. Today, everything is up for grabs: roles are shifting, rules are changing and every opinion has backers. On the one hand, we are renegotiating the structure of parenting with employers and spouses; on the other, we are adapting techniques with the benefit of new research and our own instinct for reinvention. We are doing all this in pursuit of an age-old objective: we—fathers and mothers alike—want to raise happy, curious children without fully surrendering our adult lives.

If this were ever possible, it seems so today. We are a generation that has participated in the reinvention of media, science and technology—we have cause for optimism and experience with forging new rules. Many aspects of parenting are timeless, but others have changed radically in recent decades: Fathers today spend twice as much time with their children as they did thirty years ago, for instance. More mothers are working or finding other ways to stay socially and culturally engaged. American cities are undergoing a kind of parenting renaissance—more young families are staying in cities, and as a result cities are becoming more family-friendly. And yet despite all this progress (some would say because of it), parenting remains an extremely challenging job.

The other aspect of our mission—and the closest to our hearts—is to build a community of like-minded parents. Parenting can be lonely. Together, we can connect the dots between our isolated experiences. The stories that follow are the perfect step in this process. We hope you enjoy them, and that they inspire you to share your own experiences with us at Babble.com.

— *Rufus Griscom and Alisa Volkman, co-publishers, Babble.com*

introduction

We launched Babble.com with the goal of providing new parents like us with a magazine that was smart, funny, honest and original. One of our first regular columns was called "Bad Parent," a space for parents to confess controversial parenting choices they'd made. The joke, of course, is that these days when it comes to parenting, *everything* is controversial. Whether or not you breast-feed, sleep-train, or circumcise—whatever you do with your children, someone is sure to label you a bad parent as a result.

The first installment, Jennifer Baumgardner's "How to Do Everything Wrong," began:

Conception: After psychologically disturbing visit to childhood home, solo, for holidays, have crazy, drunken break-up sex with ex-boyfriend. Don't use birth control.

The article continues through a ridiculous odyssey—a Wonder-Bra-clad delivery, dubiously successful co-parenting, and a poorly managed first day of school drop-off—but ends with a deep sense of gratitude for a child whom she loves and who loves her.

Most of the columns since have come to a similar conclusion: Whatever "mistake" was made (letting a child cry it out to fall asleep, *not* letting a child cry it out to fall asleep; going back to work right away, not going back to work at all; not having a TV, having the TV on twenty-four hours a day), we all survived it.

Whether it's resenting a stay-at-home spouse, throwing away your kid's artwork, contemplating giving away the family pets, or nursing in a moving car, all parents have done something they have mixed feelings about. But the truth is, most parents are not nearly as bad as they think they are, and there are plenty of people out there just as conflicted as them.

We started to see the column as a particularly valuable kind of service. In the magazine world, "service" refers to all those advice-y pieces like "Top Ten Ways to Help Your Teething Baby!" Those are valuable, sure, especially if it's three in the morning and you're try-ing to get your inconsolable teething baby to fall asleep. But on a spiritual level, there is something about this column that is just as useful and comforting.

These days, every parenting choice is loaded with fear—of judg-ment, of criticism, and of screwing up your kid forever. It turns out these essays provide the one thing all parents need a steady dose of—more than advice about potty-training, more than a shower, more than even a full night's sleep—reassurance that whatever they're going through, they're not alone.

As the months went by, we started to see that our "Bad Parent" columns got more traffic, and more comments, than anything else on Babble. We began offering stories on a weekly basis, and people still wanted more. Sometimes, the stories inspired condemnation: "Call CPS on this woman!" Sometimes praise: "I wish I had the courage to try this." Sometimes commiseration: "Hang in there." And always, plenty of identification: "OMG, I do this too!!!"

The wisdom and humor these writers bring to their topics reveal them to be anything *but* bad parents—they're deeply concerned about their parenting styles and the health and well-being of their families. They're making difficult choices that are right for their families, even if they're not right for everyone.

We at Babble believe that facing up to your parenting fears will actually make you a *better* parent. You'll be happier and calmer—and so will your kid. We hope you'll enjoy these stories and that they'll inspire you to let yourself and your peers off the hook. We'll all be better off if we're honest about the full range of our experiences—the good, the great, and the less than perfect.

—*Ada Calhoun, Editor-in-Chief, Babble.com*

getting something off my chest: Even I'm Freaked
Out by My Extended Breast-Feeding

Ronda Kaysen

It's two in the morning and I'm on the toilet. This would be a mundane experience if it weren't for the toddler standing beside me nursing.

My son is seventeen months old and still breast-feeds. I intended it that way. After reading oodles of attachment parenting literature, I decided that letting my child self-wean on his own time was best. What I didn't anticipate was how totally freaky and unnerving the whole experience would be.

Believe it or not, letting him suckle while I'm on the john predawn is the path of least resistance. What would happen if he didn't tag along? He would sit up in bed and scream for his "na nas," formerly known as my breasts, until they returned.

They are his breasts now. He strokes them lovingly through my shirt and cups them with his palms. He blows raspberries on them and giggles. He nurses in a toddler variation of Downward-Facing Dog while simultaneously thumbing the pages of *Goodnight Moon*. He slaps my chest with both hands and shouts, "na na! na na!" when I'm trying to discuss the finer points of a leaky faucet with the plumber. I am the body attached to his breasts.

When he displays his more theatrical nursing techniques in public or around people other than my husband, I find myself sheepish and embarrassed. I worry that someone will find this whole situation repulsive: a slapping, grunting, gulping little man waddling along beside me, clamped to my nipples.

And then I feel guilty. He's still just a baby—a very mobile baby, but a baby. And he's right to see nothing shameful or wrong about his antics. But, despite all the books and reassuring words about going at your child's pace, I can't shake the feeling that I'm judged as a weirdo because I haven't figured out how to wean this kid. I thought I'd be able to get over the cultural taboo that nursing a toddler is strange. But the scolding voices are there in my head: "A child who can walk and ask to nurse doesn't need to nurse anyway. . . . If he's old enough to unlatch your bra himself, he's too old to be doing it at all."

Sometimes the voices are sitting across from me at the dinner table. Consider this exchange from a recent luncheon with my mother and her friend at a swanky Napa, California, winery. My toddler hurdles onto my lap and nuzzles my breasts. My mom's friend, who nursed about four kids, says, "Please don't tell me you're one of those freaky Leche League moms." When I unclasp my bra, she fake shivers and shrieks, "Oh no, you are! Gross! He's got teeth!"

It wasn't always this way. Nursing the first year was bliss. I loved it. We'd lie around together for hours. He'd periodically look up at me and coo, but mostly he hummed and stayed put. In public, I tossed modesty aside and whipped out my boobs if he wanted them. If anyone looked surprised or uncomfortable, I didn't care. I was a proud breast-feeder.

"I am the body attached to his breasts."

Back then, I was nourishing a child. Now I feel like I'm entertaining one. His fascination with the outside world has eclipsed his ability to sit still long enough for the milk to arrive. Rather than wait, he rotates his body in bizarre contortions—on, say, the bus—as he tries to get a better angle or play with his toes. He is hardly subtle.

The nursing books give plenty of advice about plugged ducts, engorgement, and latching on but say little about trying to keep your dignity while your child treats your chest like a jungle gym.

La Leche League heroine Norma Jane Bumgarner comes the closest. She warns of acrobatic nursing in *Mothering Your Nursing Toddler* and suggests prohibiting your toddler from doing in private what you don't feel comfortable doing in public. If you're uncomfortable with people judging you for nursing, she says, simply dodge the "Are you still nursing?" question altogether.

I gave Bumgarner's advice a try. Here's how it went: During a recent family visit with my husband's relatives, his uncle asked, "So, does he drink his milk?" I paused for a moment. I could be truthful and say that no, we haven't introduced cow's milk, or I could just lie. But then my son solved the problem for me. He ran up to me, buried his face in my chest, and shouted, "na na!" as he yanked up my blouse.

"He's not really into cow's milk," I said, watching him latch on. He nursed for exactly fifteen seconds, long enough to make it evident that, yes, this twenty-three-pound child still nurses, but too briefly to get any nutritional benefit (or bonding benefit, for that matter) from the experience.

So, why am I still going through all this?

The World Health Organization recommends nursing for the first two years. And Dr. Sears advocates letting children self-wean. Extended nursing is nutritionally and emotionally beneficial for young children, they say. I wholeheartedly believe that. My son strokes my cheek and stops periodically to sigh in pleasure. When he's sick, it is often the only thing that makes him feel better. I can offer him this part of myself to stave off a tantrum or comfort him when he's hurt. It has benefits for me, too. When he curls up in my lap, I melt. I get to have my baby be a baby for just a little bit longer.

Recently, my son and I went to pick up vegetables at our neighborhood food co-op, which is outside a church. It was a bitterly cold November morning. As we shivered in the garden, my son asked to nurse. I turned to the pastor and asked if perhaps we could duck into his parish hall, where it was warm and quiet. He looked at me and said, "Wow, your kid will nurse in public? That's great! My wife could never get ours to nurse anywhere but in the house. It was a nightmare. She couldn't go anywhere." I'd never thought that my son's complete lack of modesty might actually be an asset.

The pastor led me inside. The church was crowded with parishioners selling Christmas wreaths and ornaments for a holiday fund-raiser. The room was full of Christmas cheer. But I was mortified. I was going to have to nurse him in front of a roomful of church ladies. "Is there a private room somewhere?" I asked. The pastor looked at me, baffled. "You could use my office, or you could nurse right here. Honestly, no one cares." It occurred to me that my fear that other people were judging me might be imagined. Maybe no one cares but me.

I ducked into the pastor's office and closed the door. The floor was covered with colorful boxes and children's toys for a holiday gift drive. My son was completely distracted by the loot. I asked him if he still wanted his "na nas." He shook his head and lunged for a truck. One day, he will stop breast-feeding altogether, and then this whole phase of parenting will be over forever. As I watched him play, I thought that maybe I should try to enjoy nursing while it lasts.

you made cereal for dinner? How I Came to Resent My Stay-at-Home Husband, and How We Got Over It

Hanna Otero

When Eric and I got married, I was six months into a preg-nancy that felt like the world's happiest accident. We had already decided that he would quit his job to care for our daughter. My publishing job offered creative freedom and a decent paycheck. Eric was still struggling to get a toehold on his culinary career. We both felt strongly that one parent should be with the baby, so this seemed an easy solution—I would make and manage the money; he would handle child care and household duties. Our new marriage was a partnership, and we felt confident that each of us would play an equal role.

For a while, it worked. Eric was a natural at fatherhood, and Madeline blossomed in his care. As much as I hated being away from my baby, knowing that she was with her dad made leaving her bearable.

Yet, even during the best days of our marriage, I felt constant pressure to bridge the gap between the countless hours Eric was able to spend with Madeline and the meager time I eked out on weekends and evenings. Even when I was exhausted, I refused to allow him to get up with the baby when she cried in the night. Those quiet moments of bonding belonged to me. I declined social invitations, afraid to miss a minute with my child—but the thought of admitting to jealousy made me feel guilty. This was the way things were, a simple fact of our lives together. Madeline was home with a parent who loved her—even if that parent wasn't me. I could live with it.

Slowly, though, things began to change. My job became less satisfying, my commute longer. We had a second baby. Eric struggled to adjust to parenting an increasingly busy three-year-old and a newborn son. I frantically juggled giving Madeline constant attention while still finding time with the baby, who was often just minutes from bedtime when I arrived home at night. Eric kept a handle on the child care, but his grasp on most other responsibilities began to slip. My work woes left me no patience for the many nights when he prepared little more than a cereal bar for dinner. We both felt overwhelmed and exhausted. Worse, we felt trapped in our roles.

In the years since Madeline's birth, my paycheck had doubled. My new salary meant a new house, one that we would not be able to afford if I quit my job. Eric could go back to work, but his comparatively modest income would barely cover the cost of child care. I felt there was no way out of a bad job; Eric felt that his return to work would be little more than a gesture—

one that would leave our kids with strangers, something neither of us wanted.

To add to the pressure, much of the nuts-and-bolts logistics of our family life still somehow ended up in my lap. I bought the birthday presents, made the doctor's appointments, organized the social calendar, and planned the vacations. I announced when it was time to buy new shoes, get our son a haircut, or join a tumbling class. I decided if we could buy that new rug or splurge on the fancy cell phones. And, to top it all off, when I was home, I insisted on calling the shots with the kids, too: no SpongeBob marathons, no sandals in November, no spaghetti and meat sauce for breakfast.

Without question, I was the boss. I believed it was because I had to be. If I didn't notice the details, Eric could go weeks or months without realizing that the baby needed a booster shot, the rugs screamed for a thorough vacuuming, and Madeline had outgrown her pants. Eric argued that I was in charge because I wanted to be. If I just got off his back, he said, he'd eventually figure it out on his own. But I could not stop myself from criticizing. I wanted my house to operate as if I were running it all the time, even if I wasn't there. I couldn't let go.

All the things that made our arrangement work in the beginning—Eric's relaxed attitude, my much more assertive approach—had slowly pushed us into our own corners. He saw me as shrill and unbending. I believed he was unmotivated and under-involved. Needless to say, we were barely civil.

Strangely, during this whole period, neither of us felt comfortable talking to anyone about how we felt. It seemed like

"I wanted my house to operate as if I were running it all the time, even if I wasn't there. I couldn't let go."

such a betrayal—and not just of one another. To let on that our gender-equal, new-millennial arrangement was falling apart felt like admitting to a much bigger failure. Besides, who among our friends could understand our points of view? My best friend is a stay-at-home mom. She identifies more with my husband's plight than she does with mine. The few women I knew in my own situation seemed, like me, unwilling to admit that things at home weren't always ideal. Unable to confront our frustrations honestly, Eric and I found ourselves going head-to-head over weighty issues, such as whose turn it was to unload the dishwasher.

Not surprisingly, things blew up. Or perhaps they melted down. Either way, we were not in a very good place when, a few months ago, we agreed to try something new. We'd sit down weekly to discuss our finances, to make a weekly menu plan, to create a family to-do list. I promised not to nag about any item on the list, as long as he promised to get things done in a timely manner. He vowed to make a meal three nights a week. We created a budget and agreed to consult one another on any nonessential purchases.

Amazingly, just this tiny, pedestrian adjustment has made a world of difference. Sunday nights, we dole out allowances in cash and discuss, item by item, where our money is going—a process that I had kept invisible to Eric for years (and, admittedly, had not always managed as well as I had pretended). Sharing that burden has been a relief. We talk about what the coming week will bring, who needs a flu shot, and when to call the electrician.

As tedious as these meetings sound, we both look forward to them. They give us a chance to talk, not just about the mundane, day-to-day matters of our life together, but about how each of us feels. We have started discussing what we might do when our debt is paid off, and how things might change if we sold the house. We are strategizing. It feels quite a lot like a business meeting between partners. It's strangely romantic.

I grew up in a military family, one where my father was deployed for weeks or months, and my mother held down whatever fort we happened to be living in at the time. Looking at my parents' marriage, I would never, ever say that one or the other of them was more essential to our survival as a family. It was only in their working together and supporting one another that they were able to support us. Isn't that the essence of marriage? And yet, I had completely lost sight of it in my own relationship.

People often remark that it takes a special kind of guy to raise children full-time. I agree completely. But it also takes a special kind of wife to concede the duties so long reserved as "mother's work" and accept that everything won't always go her way. I'm striving to be that woman, to realize that I don't get to be the domestic goddess and the financial decision-maker. Nor do I want to be, really. It's pretty clear that Eric and I need to find a new way of doing things. Perhaps in the discovery, we will invent a different marriage for ourselves.

Eric has been talking about getting back to work, taking a part-time chef gig to earn some cash and get out of the house. I am trying to think of a way to pull back on work, eliminate my commute, and spend more time with the kids. It won't happen overnight, but the belief that it could happen has given our marriage new life. In a way, we're back to where we started: a place where each of us believes that, if we work together, somehow it will all turn out just fine.

behind the curve:
I'm Embarrassed One of My Children Is "Below Average" on the Development Charts

Madeline Holler

My daughter Beatrice beat the developmental milestone charts almost every time. "Newborns smile at six weeks of age," the baby books said. Beatrice smiled in five. "Picks up small objects at the half-year mark," noted a pamphlet in the pediatrician's waiting room. She practically flicked Cheerios in the air and caught them on her tongue at five months old. Beatrice walked well before she turned one.

Experts had us expecting words around her first birthday, so my husband and I were surprised when she spoke at nine months. "Boo!" she said during peekaboo. The next day, she said, "Thank you." Soon thereafter, "Welcome." Polite too, our girl. Her contemporaries at playgroup just sat and drooled.

And why shouldn't Beatrice have been so advanced? I was doing everything right: breast-feeding exclusively, talking to her constantly. I carried her everywhere strapped to me in a sling, a crown of thorns balanced carefully on my head.

My husband and I marveled at her exceptional development and obvious intelligence. And I think we marveled a bit at ourselves: good parenting, great DNA. Let's do this again, we decided.

Here comes Frances. Or, more aptly, there she sits. Our fifteen-month-old. Not walking. Barely standing on her own. Just perched on her haunches, clapping at a pair of strappy Weeboks, still tagged and in the box. Frances has one word: "hot!" It means "scalding coffee," sure, but it also means "touch," "look," "hey!" "can I have that?" "duck," "light," and "ceiling."

Friends' children, younger than Frances, say words and perform physical feats that might as well be sonnets and high-flying acrobatics compared to my girl's. A boy in the neighborhood, born four months after her—which in baby time is like Gen Y to Frances's Gen X—runs circles around her. Literally. What does Frances do? She sits in the middle of the floor, pointing at him, saying, "hot, hot, hot!" She's a chubby-kneed Paris Hilton.

There's nothing clinically wrong with Frances. Her pediatrician is not concerned. But, according to the charts, she's below average. My child? Below average?

"Is she walking yet?" one mother at the park asked me the other day, while her younger daughter toddled toward the slides shrieking, "Up! Up!"

"She's thinking about it," I said defensively, bouncing my big girl on an aching hip. "Hot!" Frances yelled at a passing duck. Then she drooled.

"I know that each child develops in her own time.... Some babies have to be the average, or even below it. But why my daughter?"

I know the milestone charts are not there to compete against (unless your kid is winning). I know that each child develops in her own time. Realistically, some babies have to be the average, or even below it. But why my daughter?

Like everyone else who grew up watching *Oprah*, I talk a good game about personal best and individual achievements. As if being good enough is, well, good enough. The truth is: we don't celebrate the Average Joe or Jane. We're bored by Average. We pity it. We're in a world of superstars, stunning beauty, unquestionable gift, real genius. Average is bland and difficult to market; it doesn't pop on a resume. Experts and coaches and teams of handlers are hired to kick Average up a notch, to give

Average a makeover, to give it an edge. And we cringe for Below Average, which gets eliminated in the first round or swiftly voted off by its peers. Most of the time, Below Average doesn't even compete.

So, I wonder: what does this mean for my youngest daughter? What if she tracks the curve for the rest of her life? Will she even get a chance?

Let me be clear: I am not ashamed of Frances. She's Kewpie doll cute and deliciously roly-poly. She isn't, euphemistically speaking, slow. She has a clever sense of humor, albeit subtly and wordlessly expressed. (The way she circles her index finger across the colored pages of *Goodnight Moon* pretending to search diligently for the mouse, for example.) Plus, she's my kid! Mine! Of course, I'm proud of my big, fat toddler with weak legs, bad balance! Her mum's-the-word policy just indicates a trustworthiness to come! (Or am I being defensive?)

Still, a confession: I have winced more than once at the . . . how shall I say it? . . . *casual* pace of her development. Not because of what it may say about her; rather, what it says about me. When my patient, schedule-imposing, by-the-baby-book friend's daughter sat her fourteen-month-old self down for fake tea and some girl talk while the older Frances flung *Touch and Feel: Kitten* books around the room, I considered the contrast between the two girls an indictment of my parenting, the loose structure of our household, my inability to keep to any kind of feeding/sleeping/park-visiting schedule.

My niece could manage sleepovers away from her mother when she was just a couple of months old. Not my Frances. Even after more than a year, she wakes up in the middle of the night looking for me. Is that normal? Should she be doing overnights? Are my expectations too low? Too high? Do I nurse her too much? Do I hold her too much? Ignore her too much? Pay attention too much? Should I have done something differently when she was an infant? Should I change something now? Should I have spent my pregnancy listening to Mozart or eating line-caught salmon and sautéed greens instead of watching back-to-back episodes of *Law & Order* and knocking back a plate of brownies every night? Why, oh why, is my baby such a baby? Is this really her personal best? (Is it mine?)

I could get her some outside help and sign up for so-called enrichment classes, I suppose. Some Mommy and Me Science Walks (I'll carry her), a season of Kindermusik classes with supplemental Baby Einstein tapes at home. I could crib a pre-K lesson plan from some do-it-yourself preschool Web site or read up on self-direction techniques from the Montessorians. But that sounds like a lot of work. Sure, I would meet other parents who are also in a quiet panic about their children's intelligence and, therefore, future. We could commiserate and compare notes. But I already regularly run into a mother who "works on colors" with her twenty-month-old and is training her disinterested three-year-old to read. Her fervor is draining, as is the fear that I should be doing that, too. And let's face it: when she starts school, Frances could very well be the worst in the class. Then what would I do?

Another option is to quit wincing, hide my concern, get over myself, and stop worrying. So, she's developmentally average, or even below it. She can make up for it in other ways: kindness, grace, a total and unshakable indifference to what other people think of her.

Maybe my babe will show some pluck and kick other kids' asses in long division or dodgeball (I just hope it's not when she's sixteen and the other kids are six). In any case, I should keep my gaze on her and ignore charts that determine how she sizes up with her age group. I should stop scanning her big sister's baby book to see how they compare. I am not a judge, or a fellow castaway, or a member of the audience. I am her mother. And what I really want for her—for Beatrice, too—is that she achieve her personal best without regard to her peers or how it plays to a focus group, college admissions staff, or even her insecure and impatient mother.

Of course, Frances will walk some day, probably soon. Eventually, she'll add "cold" to her lexicon. But Frances is developing in Frances-time into the Frances she will inevitably be.

I'll just wait.

diamonds are for labor: I Succumbed to the Push Present Craze

Jennifer Blaise Kramer

The names alone are pretty crass: push present, push prize, baby bauble, baby mama gift. They all refer to the jewelry (or in some cases, the top-of-the-line handbags) a husband is supposed to give his wife after she gives birth. Often, men have never heard of this rite until they're warned not to show up to the delivery room without something glittering in hand.

The first time I heard of the concept was about five years ago. The story was actually quite endearing. A friend had an emergency C-section, and the doctor told her to remove all her jewelry so it wouldn't need to be cut off if the swelling got bad. Two days and one healthy baby girl later, her husband returned bearing take-out and a sweet surprise. He put on her wedding rings and then slipped on another he'd had made to match the wedding band, with diamonds all around. She was floored. I could see why.

But, as the years passed, the story got a little old. And so did my other friends' similar stories: another baby, another diamond. Once, I met a friend-turned-mother for lunch and she came walking up, smiling into the carriage. I oohed and aahed over the newborn. Then my friend flashed her newly acquired third ring, as if expecting just as much enthusiasm.

"I felt more than ever that it was high time for something shiny."

Suddenly, the idea seemed so contrived. As if I'd be waiting to hear what my friends got—a ring, a watch, earrings for twins—rather than whether they'd had a boy or a girl. And while a token of appreciation for carrying a child seems sweet, I started feeling bad for the guys. Gone was the simplicity I'd imagined, the bouquet of flowers or the pink or blue balloons on the mailbox. This push present phenomenon puts dads-to-be in a tricky predicament; if they don't get her anything, they're insensitive or cheap, and if they do, they're a cliché, just checking off a box on a to-do list.

I shared my irritation about the matter with my husband. He seemed relieved and agreed it felt a little forced.

When my time rolled around a couple of years later, I reminded my husband not to get caught up in the push present peer pressure, even though hauling around an extra fifty pounds in the tenth month made me wonder if a medal would be out of the question.

In those final weeks, I was having lunch with some fellow pregnant women from my prenatal yoga class and commented on a friend's stunning antique ring. Turns out it was her push present for her first child. She'd eyed it for years, and once the baby was born her husband surprised her with it. She couldn't help but wonder what he might do for the pending number two.

Some at the table confessed that they, too, were hoping for something sparkly after the birth and had started dropping hints to their husbands months before. But others thought the whole phenomenon was ridiculous. One woman snapped that a beautiful, healthy baby should be reward enough. The prize is the baby, not the bauble, she reminded the rest of us with scorn. She talked as if the bejeweled were a bunch of "bridezillas," who obsess over the wedding and forget about the marriage part.

That's what I'd thought until that moment, but suddenly she seemed like a spoilsport. I started to think that such gorgeous gifts were not ridiculous, but fitting markers for a new phase in life. Much like the wedding band is a symbol of marriage, the push present is a tangible way to document another major milestone.

When I finally had my baby—after extreme nausea, midnight vomiting, swollen legs, sleepless nights, breath-stopping contractions, and a labor that lasted days—I felt more than ever that it was high time for something shiny. And when my husband said he wanted us to go shopping together for a pendant of the baby's birthstone, citrine, I didn't fight him. It would be something special that we could give to our daughter on her sixteenth birthday.

He called a jewelry store, asking if they had a nice selection of citrine; they said no, and added that he should really consider diamonds. The jewelry industry now has yet another niche, selling birth like a Hallmark holiday, with a side order of guilt. Some retailers even have "new mom" registries, removing the last ounce of romance from the process.

Instead, my husband hung up, and we went together, pushing the baby carriage downtown, in search of citrine. We found a lovely drop pendant with matching stud earrings. I wore them to a Christmas party, on our first night away from the baby, and I found myself reaching for them, a subtle reminder of our baby back at home. For me, this "push present" is a memento of all the bliss and anxiety of those first days. Such a monumental event is worth making a fuss over, even in a material way. If only it had a less graphic name.

out of sight:
Why I Don't Use a Baby Monitor

Elizabeth Blackwell

A few years ago, I checked in with a friend who'd been having a tough time with her high-maintenance newborn. "I don't even eat until after my husband comes home," I remember her moaning. "Whenever I put the baby down to fix something, he cries."

In deference to her hormonal hysteria, I refrained from sharing my immediate reaction: So?

As a new mom, I regularly left my daughter to shriek in her bouncy seat while I scarfed down my lunch or took a shower. Occasional neglect seemed like a relatively minor maternal sin, especially since it was the only way I got anything done around the house. Wasn't it in my daughter's best interest to ensure our toilets weren't condemned by the Health Department?

I developed a habit of lolling around bed in the morning, not responding to my daughter's cries down the hall until they progressed from gentle mewling to outright fury. And in that spirit, I refused to buy a baby monitor.

These days, it seems, there's no such thing as an off-duty parent. Even when your children are sleeping, you must remain tethered to them by an electronic gadget, one of those modern-parenting must-haves that our own parents somehow survived without.

Initially, my husband and I assumed we'd buy a monitor; that we didn't have one by the time Clara came home from the hospital was a result of disorganization more than anything else. (We were the parents who neglected to pack a "going home" outfit for our newborn and stared in stunned horror at the nurse when we were being discharged, terrified we'd be sent out the door with a naked baby.)

As the months passed, we realized we didn't miss having a monitor, and we remained monitor-less even after twin boys arrived a few years later. We live in a two-story, 1950s suburban house. When there's a real emergency in the kids' rooms upstairs (e.g., someone's chubby leg jammed in between the crib rails), the screaming carries to our family room downstairs and we head up to investigate. What we can't hear is every little whimper and wail, those distracting sounds that can send your heart thumping in *she's-not-sleeping-yet-please-God-go-to-sleep* panic.

Studio-apartment-dwellers aside, we're clearly in the minority with our no-monitor stance. On those rare occasions that we hang out with fellow parents in the evening or during afternoon naptime, there's almost always a monitor lurking on a side table, a reminder that the kids are with us even when they aren't. The monitor utters a low, steady hiss, a combination of static and indistinguishable baby noises, a distraction that prevents us from ever completely relaxing. *In this house, the kid rules*, it seems to be saying.

"... there's no such thing as an off-duty parent."

I'm all for checking in on your kids, and I do make several trips upstairs each night to make sure everyone's okay (or, during those early months, to check that everyone's still breathing). So, maybe I do more schlepping up and down than people who have a monitor. But it's worth it, and not just because I count it as my daily cardio. For a few precious hours, my husband and I revert to our previous, laid-back selves, rather than haggard parents second-guessing every noise our new masters make.

As the years have passed, I've gotten more reckless, venturing out to the backyard during naptime. On the off chance the boys woke up early, I wouldn't hear them, but what's the worst that could happen? They're in cribs, in a childproofed room with the door closed. Will there really be any long-term damage if they have to wallow a little longer in a skanky diaper? Possibly, but it'll be a good ten years or so before they start laying down the guilt trips.

When I get a break from my children, I take it—not just physically but mentally. I remember watching an *Oprah* segment about moms in Iceland leaving their bundled-up babies outside in strollers while they gathered inside a cozy café for coffee and chitchat. Did I mention that this was during the winter? In Iceland?

I don't think I'd ever be that bold—besides, pulling that stunt during a Midwestern January might get me arrested. But I think there's something to be said about having your kids nearby, yet not too close. For allowing them some space, even when they're babies. For putting them to bed, and then leaving them alone.

Eight o'clock is the magic hour in my house, the time I tell the kids, who are now six and two, that Mommy stops working. Once they're in bed, I don't really care what they do, as long as they're breathing and eventually sleeping. Without a baby monitor picking up their every twitch, they're free to do as they like. And, more importantly, so am I.

mama's boys:
Am I Spoiling My Sons?

Emily Mendell

The enormity of my predicament hit me like a Tonka truck
last winter as I was navigating the normal morning tumult of
getting my boys ready for school. To speed along the process of
getting dressed, I had come up with the nifty idea of running
their clothes through the dryer for about a minute. It worked
brilliantly. The clothes came out all toasty, and the boys couldn't
get that underwear on fast enough! But, one day, several weeks
into this routine, the dryer was full of wet laundry and the boys
had to (*gasp*) put on room-temperature clothing.

They whined: "I can't wear these pants. My shirt isn't warm.
You *have* to warm up these clothes."

As I began lightheartedly pulling the soppy clothes out of
the dryer so that my boys could have warm socks, I was suddenly crippled by horrific visions of my sweet little sons at age

thirty, griping to their wives that they needed their clothes to be warmed each morning because that's what their mother did for them.

Oh my god, I thought, *I'm raising mama's boys.* I had mysteriously grown apron strings, despite the fact that I don't cook.

Before my husband and I had children, it was assumed by all who knew us that when we became parents, I would be the bad cop. Call central casting for the disciplinarian, and I would be the first sent down. While I was a type A, stick-to-the-rules, eat-what-you-kill kind of gal, my husband was incredibly laid-back. Nothing seemed to bother him. Ever. Even I was certain that our future children would figure out quickly that when Mommy says no, Daddy will say yes. But it didn't turn out that way at all.

Within twenty-six months, I gave birth to two little boys and transformed into a completely different person. I became extremely proficient at nurturing my sons and fairly impotent at disciplining them. To this day, I am the first to cave on punishments and the last to say no to double dessert.

Don't like what we are having for dinner? No problemo! I'll fix you something special.

You just earned a thirty-minute time-out, mister! Okay, maybe fifteen minutes. Alright, six, but that is it!

I see that Lego set costs $49.99. How much do you have? Alright, I'll make up the extra $42.

Even worse, I actually enjoy doing things for the boys that they should clearly be doing for themselves. Somewhere deep inside, fixing snacks, making beds, packing schoolbags, combing hair, and picking out clothes makes me feel happy and motherly.

"I had mysteriously grown apron strings, despite the fact that I don't cook."

Meanwhile, my husband, Mr. Mellow, has slipped easily into the role of authoritarian. He used to just roll his eyes at my indulgences, but lately he's been pushing back.

What he wants to know is this: why would a woman who is hardwired for dealing with the world in a certain manner undergo a complete personality change when dealing with her children? Does the fact that I am the only female in my house have something to do with it? Could there be unknown forces at work here?

While it would be convenient to blame my over-mothering entirely on chromosomes, I know better. Not all mothers of boys are, like me, in favor of the "seventeen strikes and you're out" rule. Some don't even offer second chances. Here, according to the experts, is where our pasts come into play big-time.

"Because they have never been boys themselves, mothers project a great deal of their own experiences with men onto their sons," says Michael Thompson, PhD, author of *It's a Boy!*

Understanding Your Son's Development from Birth to Age 18 and the *New York Times* best seller *Raising Cain: Protecting the Emotional Life of Boys*. "If they look at their sons and see in them a loving grandfather, father, or brother it is tremendously positive, but if they view an ex-husband or an abusive boyfriend, it can be quite the opposite. We all project our biggest disappointments and greatest happiness on the opposite gender."

So, for my award-winning role as doormat, I would like to thank my father, who was largely absent during my teen years, as well as boyfriends #1, 3, 4, and 6 for inspiring me to please my little men at all costs. Without those male influences, I never would have been able to cut up the meat of an eleven-year-old boy with such genuine enthusiasm.

Thankfully, I'm not a lost cause. According to Dr. Thompson, the one thing keeping me from being totally overbearing and creepy is the fact that I grew up with a normal kid brother who evolved into a fully functioning adult. Without that experience, I might worry much more about my boys.

"Mothers who grew up with brothers tend to have faith that everything will be okay," says Dr. Thompson.

This faith is born out of the experience of watching brothers go through their natural stages of development, including those wild and weird stages, and having it all work out in the end.

Despite the genetic and psychological rationales for my mothering style, the fifty-million-dollar question remains: Is my close, enabling relationship with my boys too much?

"Every boy has his mother to thank for his emotional foundation," says Dr. Thompson. "A mother has tremendous psychological power. But, as he grows, a boy must be able to leave his mother without losing her completely and return to her without losing himself."

At some point, and that point is rapidly approaching, I will begin to cut my apron strings, not all at once, but thread by thread. I'm counting on my boys to give me some clues about when, and which ones to cut first. The clothes-in-the-dryer trick is largely a thing of the past. And, this year, I resolved to stop laying out their clothes for them and hovering over their homework. Still, I hope even when they grow more independent, we will remain connected for life. And if they ever need a little extra warmth, they'll know where to find it.

the minimalist:
I Don't Buy My Kid Toys

Nan Mooney

Last week I took Leo, my eight-month-old son, on a playdate, and we decided to give his friend Cameron's Exersaucer a trial run. Watching that huge smile as he pedaled his feet and banged on the plastic piano keys, I felt a not unfamiliar pang of guilt.

Leo doesn't have an Exersaucer. Or a Jumperoo. He doesn't have portable spoons and snack jars or a Peapod tent for napping on the road. He doesn't even have a nursery. He sleeps in a crib an arm's length from my bed, and his changing table consists of a hand towel spread across the foot of that same bed.

Partly by choice and partly of necessity, I'm raising my son in a very minimalist style. I'm a single mother, temporarily residing in an apartment in my parents' basement. We don't have much space or money, so he doesn't have much stuff. I'm also a firm believer in doing all I can to fight the "you are what you own" messages that flood our kids the second they walk out the front door.

In part, I'm proud to invest him with nonmaterialistic values. But at times I feel guilty, too. I'm not entirely convinced that never having a slate of developmental toys, a library full of books, or a fancy birthday party won't actually hurt him in some way. What if, in my efforts to pare down, I neglect to provide Leo with some crucial item that really would make him a happier, more successful, more well-rounded kid?

When I browse the Pottery Barn Kids catalog or spot a Bugaboo on the street, I feel pretty confident. Leo will turn out just fine without those things. But the border between want and need isn't always so clear. Earlier this summer, Leo and I took a trip to the East Coast and stayed for a couple of weeks with friends, intellectuals who share my minimalist parenting philosophy. Toys hadn't consumed their apartment, but it did contain stack upon teetering stack of children's books in four languages.

"We don't spend on clothes or toys," my friend explained. "But we do buy books. We're language people, and we feel like that's a critical part of education."

Again the wash of guilt. I'm a language person, too. Will reading Leo the same ten board books we inherited from a friend somehow stymie him intellectually? My friends' two-year-old daughter is, indeed, breathtakingly precocious, bilingual and already working on language number three. I came home from that trip twenty dollars poorer for having invested in a pair of French children's books that, so far, Leo's only tried to eat.

More often than I'd like to admit, my reluctance to spend money on my child leaves me feeling embarrassed and a little ashamed. I don't want to become one of those "no" parents—no TV, no sugar, no spontaneous trips to the zoo. Nor do I want Leo's memories of childhood to be defined by what he didn't have or do. And always swirling out there is the inference, real or imagined, that if I don't buy Leo this or that toy or piece of equipment or learning experience, I'm a bad parent. When a close friend with two older daughters sends me Craigslist postings for used toys, is it pure helpfulness or is it undergirded by a message that I'm not adequately nurturing my child? I know I've covered the basics: food, clothing, diapers, and a place to lay his head. But, beyond that, what do kids really need to make them centered and successful?

Right now, Leo is pretty happy banging measuring spoons and sucking his toes. He seems just as precocious and delightful as his more advantaged peers, even his friend Sonya, who has a computerized pet dog that takes photos. It's the parents, not the babies, who are caught up in a flurry of swimming lessons, baby joggers, and Mozart for Children CDs.

But, as he gets older, I know the questions will get trickier. I grew up an only child in a comfortably middle-class family. I didn't have it as good as the girl down the street with a miniature car she drove up and down her driveway, but there were always plenty of presents under the Christmas tree and games in the game cupboard. My best friend was the youngest of four, and I still remember the searing jealousy she couldn't manage to suppress as I got skating lessons and new clothes while she was stuck with hand-me-downs. Will Leo experience that same kind

"... my reluctance to spend money on my child leaves me feeling embarrassed and a little ashamed."

of resentment toward kids who have more? How will he cope with the sense of being on the outside looking in?

I suppose this balancing of wants versus needs marks a line he and I will always walk together. I will give him all that I can. But, in my mind, providing for your child means, first and foremost, imbuing him with a sense of compassion, tolerance, trust in and pleasure with the world around him. I suppose that eventually reality will do its damnedest to show him different. But, for as long as possible, I plan to preserve in him the belief that love really is all you need.

supersize me:
I Feed My Baby Fast Food

Jennifer Blaise Kramer

I swore I'd never turn into a hermit when I had a baby, reassuring myself that we'd still go out to dinner. I was terrified of living—and eating—vicariously through friends. Once pregnant, I tuned out other parents who said they couldn't remember the last movie they'd seen in the theater and hadn't heard of any of the new restaurants we'd mention. They'd tell us to live it up while we could because, once the baby came, we'd lose our freedom. On some level, I knew it just didn't have to be this way.

Since part of my job used to be reviewing restaurants, and I'd put in my time as a server, I wanted our daughter to grow up around a variety of foods and with a respect for the restaurant business. I remember a couple of encouraging chefs (ones with kids) saying that new parents should keep frequenting their favorite neighborhood restaurants, just go earlier and eat quicker (e.g., order wines by the glass, and skip the cheese course).

Determined, we took our Stella out when she was four days old, starting with a trip to Starbucks. Since that went so well, we spent the following months introducing her to all sorts of places and ethnic foods, even if she merely watched from her little bucket seat. We did the taquerias, where lively Mexican music made a nice backdrop to the meltdowns (tip: never, ever leave the pacifier at home). We hit the Irish pubs, sipping Guinness while the proprietor congratulated us for starting her early. And we adored Italian, given they're the same lovely people who poured me wine without asking when I was pregnant, God love them.

Around the three-month mark, I met a friend at a local coffee shop, one that prides itself on being the anti-Starbucks, selling whole-grain goodies and swirling foam designs into their lattes. It was packed with the usuals—designers, hipsters, students, writers—all eyeing me as I settled in with my small cappuccino and rather less small stroller, which required major maneuvering to squeeze it out of the walkway.

Stella started moaning and tossing toys aside anxiously, so I began to mix up a bottle, fumbling with the formula. My friend nervously offered to hold the baby, now turning red in the face with impatient hunger cries. Someone bumped into the stroller while I tore apart my diaper bag for a burp cloth, and the water and coffee spilled along with a mess of napkins onto the floor. Every face turned toward me with irritated and annoyed smirks. I felt like Julia Roberts in *Pretty Woman*—*You're obviously in the wrong place, pleeaase leave!*

To give a nod to the pros who had warned us it'd be tough, it got worse when we had to swap the infant carrier for a high chair. Suddenly, we required special furniture and, more importantly, an extra-tolerant environment. When blood sugar runs low in our household, we call it "Feed the beast!" and our baby in her pre-Cheerio state is no exception.

When the beast came out during a recent road trip, we ducked into a McDonald's for the first time since getting scared straight by *Fast Food Nation*. It was instant gratification without the agony of waiting. I indulged in chicken nuggets and fries. So did Stella. She squealed with delight, which brought smiles, not stares, to the faces around us. I pushed aside her organic applesauce and semisoft cheese and let her get all greasy. Memories of sitting there with my mom and my grandma came flooding back, and I felt strangely proud.

For better or for worse, perhaps for pure convenience, McDonald's will always be a rite of passage. It's often how kids think of a restaurant—fun, friendly, colorful, and not pretentious. It's so refreshing to hear kids say, "chicken nuggets" or "hot dogs," when asked about their favorite foods. With all the pressure to be all-natural all the time, I get nervous a little three-year-old will respond "edamame" or "tofu pups." I really worry for the tiny tot who might mechanically utter the word "organic" as if it's a singular food on its own.

With so much emphasis on going organic early, we're so afraid of pesticides in the fruit we puree and hormones in the beef we cook that it can be pretty scary to leave home, unless it's just a quick jaunt to Whole Foods. Unfortunately, the same restaurants that support all-natural, sustainable farming don't

"The chain of all restaurant chains is still super baby-friendly, with its heaps of high chairs and Happy Meals."

really cater to kids. Last weekend, I called an old local favorite, and while they said they welcomed children, they had to put me on hold to ask if they had high chairs.

I can't blame these places for holding up a certain standard. When I'm at a nice restaurant, paying those prices, I expect a certain level of service and presentation. It just doesn't work with a mac-and-cheese-smeared baby, dropping toys and food on the ground while the server plays defense, moving back wine and water glasses and shuffling hot plates to safety zones. It isn't fair to other diners, and it's not fair to the restaurateurs, whose crisp vision of a dining experience—complete with soft music, white porcelain, and sparkling stemware—does not come with baby.

It's a lot like the local bookshops and boutiques we try so hard to support, only to find our stroller doesn't quite fit down the aisle, our item isn't in stock, and our crying baby has totally interrupted their vibe. It puts us parents who previously avoided the big-box and fast-food world in quite a predicament. Do we choose independent or convenient? Healthy or friendly? We don't have the time we once did to browse shops, read menus, and hop all over town to find what we want. McDonald's—much like those evil big-box retailers—gets this. They always have.

The chain of all restaurant chains is still super baby-friendly, with its heaps of high chairs and Happy Meals. True to its genre, it is quick, which we frantic parents appreciate, as well as clean and affordable. And despite what snobs (and maybe Morgan Spurlock) say, the food will not kill you. We should give them some credit for stepping into the twenty-first century with healthier options like all-white-meat chicken, salads, and apple slices. Now they're even making lattes. It almost makes me want to carry one into my cranky coffee shop, stroller first, and say, "Remember me? I was in here yesterday, and you wouldn't wait on me? Big mistake. Big! Huge!"

Maybe it's time for the indies to take a cue from the chains and make some room for the stroller set. Or at least not be so judgmental when it comes to fast food. It's nice to have a place where no one flinches when families walk in mid-meltdown and where grandparents giggle watching babies taste French fries for the first time. Personally, I find it comforting that my post-preschool hangout is here for my daughter's generation and feel like giving Mickey D's a little pat on the back for modernizing themselves. So, until there's a place with organic food that supports sustainable farming that's open twenty-four hours a day (or at least for lunch!), I certainly won't be boycotting the Golden Arches.

unschooling: I'm Not
Sending My Five-Year-Old to School This Year—
or Maybe Ever

Joanne Rendell

My son, Benny, was out late last night at a bar in SoHo.
It's now 10:30 AM, and he's spread-eagled across his bed, one
long leg dangling off the mattress. His dirty bangs hang over
his closed eyes; his mouth flutters open and shut as he breathes
deep, sleeping breaths. As ever, his socks are on, threadbare and
gray at the heels.

In this pose, he's an average teenage boy, except for two things:
he's just shy of five years old, and today he starts un-kindergarten.

It's the new school year, and while Benny's been sleeping this
morning, many of his old babyhood friends have already eaten
breakfast, donned their shining new backpacks and shoes, and
trooped off toward their very first day of kindergarten.

Benny knows the word *kindergarten*. He's read about kids
going to such a place in his books, many of which he insists on

"We have no lesson plans drawn up for the coming year. We've ordered no curricula."

reading on his own these days. But he hasn't yet asked if he will be going to kindergarten. My partner, Brad, and I haven't really mentioned that he won't be.

Benny's never heard of un-kindergarten though. That's because I made up the term last night.

We were out with friends having drinks. Benny was with us, as usual. We'd hit that lull time around nine o'clock, post–happy hour and pre–late night revelers, when New York City bartenders don't seem to mind five-year-olds playing with cars and sipping cranberry juice near the bar.

Our friends have no kids but were curious about our decision not to send Benny to school. They're aware enough to know that homeschooling is no longer (and probably never was) just a bunch of Bible-thumping Seventh Day Adventists, who teach their kids at home in order to avoid the heathens at public school. Our friends also understand that parents homeschool their kids in different ways and for different reasons.

Nonetheless, when I used the term "unschooling," they needed an explanation.

"There's no good sound bite to describe it," I said, "just as there's no good sound bite to describe school. But, generally speaking, unschoolers don't send their kids to regular school and avoid teaching by curriculum. You won't find them at the kitchen table every morning doing math, then reading, then geography."

I went on to explain that unschoolers believe in letting children's curiosity, interests, and natural hunger for knowledge guide their learning.

"So, are you unschoolers, then?" Julie, our friend, asked.

Brad and I exchanged glances, then gave vague yes/no head waggles.

On the homeschool spectrum, we're probably nearer to the unschool end—at least, for the time being. We have no lesson plans drawn up for the coming year. We've ordered no curricula. The way we helped Benny learn to read was very ad hoc and unstructured. (He liked road signs a lot, so we started with the words *bump, stop, yield, ahead* and went from there.)

Neither of us has ever read a word of John Holt—the grand master of the unschooling world who, apparently, wrote both about the failure of schools and the importance of teaching kids how to learn instead of what to learn. Nor do we believe that unschooling is necessarily the only and best way for every child to be educated.

Moreover, to call ourselves unschoolers seems so definitive and final; I'm not sure whether in two, or five, or ten years' time, an unschooling, laissez-faire approach to Benny's education will work for our family.

That's when I came up with my new term.

"He's going to un-kindergarten this year, that's for sure," I joked with our friends last night, before ordering us all another beer and Benny another cranberry juice.

On our first un-kindergarten day, Benny got up at noon, a little later than his usual 11 AM start. I worked on my latest novel while he slept, as I always do. Brad, who's a professor at NYU, headed out to teach his first class of the semester.

After he got up, Benny spent an hour playing a complicated game that involved five toy cars and a couple of bungee cords. Then we headed over to Brooklyn on the subway, stopping in Chinatown on the way to pick up fresh fruit and rice snacks. Benny delighted in counting out four quarters to pay a stall owner for some bananas.

Now, in the warm afternoon sun, Benny is playing with two other kids in a strip of mud in a small backyard. His two friends are completely naked. Benny has on his underpants and a pair of socks. Almost every inch of childish skin, cotton, and hair is covered with wet, sticky dirt. The kids are completely absorbed in the task at hand: burying a bobble-eyed baby doll in the dirt. At the moment, the doll's torso and legs are completely submerged. Her head is exposed, but one eyelid is held down by mud. An earthworm wriggles just a couple of inches away from the doll's shining plastic scalp.

The whole scene could be a performance art piece or perhaps an excerpt from a very twisted movie about child killers. Instead, this is just an average day at the new little homeschool/ unschool/DIY-preschool playgroup we attend each week.

"... Benny is not at 'real' kindergarten today because that is what suits my family at this moment."

While Benny and his coconspirators work on their burial project, other kids in the yard are also busy. One is fiddling with the brake system on a tricycle. Another is feeding a carrot to a rather worried pet rabbit. Two little girls are dancing, fully clothed, in a sprinkler.

We mothers and one father sit nearby drinking cool beer. Many of us have been away during the summer, and we're celebrating being back together again. We are a ragtag bunch: writers, artists, actors, an activist, one doula, and a carpenter. Our kids' ages range from one to six.

As the baby doll takes her last one-eyed glimpse of daylight and the bunny retreats to his hutch, our conversation turns to the "whole school thing." It's the first day of school for the rest of the country.

Some of the group are die-hard unschoolers. They believe the current school system deadens young minds and that there is nothing worse for developing curiosity and self-learning than an overworked teacher spooning out knowledge in bite-size chunks. The schoolhouse, they believe, is a "cage," and the only way to teach kids how to be and learn in the world is to take them out into it.

Others of us are on the fence. One mom has decided not to send her kids to preschool this year but is still open to the idea of kindergarten next year. Another mom has twin sons in first grade at a public school but has decided not to send her younger child to preschool; she hopes one day to homeschool all three.

A few of us like the idea of some sort of curriculum, or at the very least adding more structured activities, such as reading circles or science experiments, into our weekly meetings. One member of the group has already ordered a number of home-school curricula online, and she and her son are very active in New York's vibrant homeschool community.

As we talk, I realize that Benny is not at "real" kindergarten today because that is what suits my family at this moment. I'm not against school. Not by any means. After all, Brad and I fared pretty nicely after a regular school education. With two PhDs between us and a couple of published books, our desire to learn clearly wasn't quashed.

But un-kindergarten for us means Benny can sleep late so I can write. It means we don't have to worry about bedtimes and can go out on the town with friends any night of the week. We can go to Europe and visit my family when the flights are cheap. Un-kindergarten also means we can pick and choose how we spend our days and with whom we spend them. Benny can go to free classes at the Metropolitan Museum of Art during the week, when it's less crowded. He can read a book on sharks when he feels like it. He can experiment with bungee cords while eating his breakfast at noon.

By the end of the afternoon, baby doll is finally sealed in her earthy tomb, and the kids have been hosed down with cold water. Their shrieks are heard across Brooklyn. Benny and I will now head back to Manhattan, reading the subway signs along the way ("DO NOT LEAN ON DOOR"; "NO EXIT").

Tonight, we will meet Brad for dinner and go see a movie at the theater. Benny's not into kid flicks like *Finding Nemo* or *Monsters, Inc.* They scare him silly. *Juno* was Benny's favorite this year. He likes to say, when he sees a pregnant woman, "She looks like a planet."

After the movie, we'll head home, read books, and fall asleep around midnight. Our first day of un-kindergarten will be done, and we'll sleep well knowing that Benny is learning, growing, and enjoying his five-year-old, mud-splattered life, even in the absence of workbooks, fingerpaints, and school bells.

clothing optional:
I Let My Daughter Run Around Naked

Ellen Friedrichs

Aside from streaking on a dare at sixteen and attending an
"underwear" party a number of years back, I can't claim to have
had a lot of experience with public nudity. My two-year-old daughter, Clementine, on the other hand, is already making quite an
impression in the parks we frequent by doffing her clothes at
every opportunity.

The first time I got a comment about this, I was more star-
tled than anything. We were in a local Brooklyn playground.
Clem was one. The place was practically deserted, and she was
naked, playing in a sprinkler.

I noticed a cop stroll in and talk to an older couple sitting at
the opposite side of the park. A few minutes later he strolled over
to me. "Do you speak Polish?" he asked.

"No. Sorry," I told him.

"I'm trying to tell them they can't be in here without a child, but they don't understand." He paused for a second. "You know, you really should put some clothes on your baby. People like that, you can't always trust them."

At first I was a little surprised. The old folks—who seemed simply to be having lunch—were potential pedophiles? I would have never guessed. *Good thing I'm not a cop,* I thought.

It seemed more likely that the couple simply hadn't understood the sign that read *All adults must be accompanied by a child.* He paused. I mumbled something about how it was fine with me if they stayed and that I would keep an eye on Clem.

"They're lucky," he told me. "You saved them a ticket. But you really should put something on your daughter."

I didn't, and as a result I spent the rest of the time we were there worried that the cop would come back and haul me away.

Other incidents have been less amicable, and now that I have a two-year-old, they have also become more common. That's because the two-year-old in question could pass for three and sees no need to stay dressed when it's hot. Or when she's bored. Or if there's water anywhere in sight. Or just because.

That "just because" was the catalyst for a recent comment we got as we walked into our building. To me, a toddler in a Onesie is fully dressed, but a woman in the foyer disagreed. "Looks like someone forgot her pants today," she said. I couldn't quite read her tone, yet I felt defensive. "She had a skirt," I said too quickly. "But she took it off."

Just because.

It's funny: despite hearing tongue-clucking and getting vaguely accusatory questions from other parents ("Don't you worry about people looking at her when she's not wearing anything?" "Did you see there are boys here, too?"), I have yet to hear the most obvious and legitimate argument for clothing a baby: accidents.

That's the one I really worry about. (Next in line: sunburns. We are of pasty stock.) Clementine has been on the cusp of being toilet trained for longer than I would like. We have good days and bad. The possibility of her pooping in a playground seems a lot more dangerous than the possibility that she will incite someone to child molestation.

Of course, I know for some parents the issue is decorum. I overheard one mom telling her three-year-old that she needed to wear a bathing suit "because of modesty." And I do respect that, in many cultures, nudity just is not seen as acceptable at any age. The thing is: in mine, it is.

It's not that I'm a radical when it comes to parenting. Clem's been vaccinated, nursed for only six months, and drinks from sippy cups that I am sure leach BPA. But I am all for allowing her to drop her drawers whenever she likes.

I have this idea that the more I let her be naked now, the more accepting of her body she will be later. I don't know that any studies would back me up. At this point, it's just a hunch. And it's a hope, grown out of a decade spent working with teenage girls who hate their bodies, that somehow my kid will be an exception.

But I'm not about to get into this when I am told by a stranger to dress her.

The most recent incident took place at another Brooklyn park. We were returning from a doctor's appointment and spied

the enticing combination of kids, swings, and spurting foun-
tains. So, we detoured. Everyone else seemed to have the proper
gear: swim diapers, water shoes, and buckets. The fact that we
didn't wasn't about to stop Clem, who promptly raced into the
fray. Realizing she was soaked, she began to strip down. I helped
pull her out of a tangled tank top, collected her sodden diaper,
and stepped back to observe.

"I have this idea that the more I let her be naked now, the more accepting of her body she will be later."

Apparently, I wasn't the only one watching, and within
seconds I heard a sharp admonishment. "That's your daughter?
You have to put clothes on her!" It was the keeper of the park,
a man who was identified by a sign hanging over the bath-
rooms as Louis. By this time, I had done a little "research"—
if you call trolling neighborhood parenting Listservs and
clicking through the NYC Parks Web site research. The latter

wasn't helpful. But if my fellow parents—the ones who also let their kids go nude and who claimed to have actually called the park's manager about this issue—were to be believed, then there were no specific rules on the subject of baby nakedness.

Even so, I told Louis, "Okay, I'll put a diaper on her in a sec."

I received a stern reply. "She can't just wear a diaper. You have to dress her."

In a city where adult women have legally been able to walk around topless since 1992, this seemed a little odd.

"Actually, I don't. That's not in the rules," I answered, feeling defiant. But because I have a weird respect for even the lowest forms of authority, I only let Clem splash for another minute before collecting our stuff, wrangling her into half an outfit, and walking out.

Because, really, if my motivation for letting her run around with a bare butt is that I don't want to make a big deal of her nudity, then it would be kind of counterproductive to cause a scene by using her as a naked pawn in my body-acceptance crusade.

For now, Clem can run free. Until we get called out. Then I guess I'll put a diaper on her. And soon: underwear. That will be an exciting day. Almost as exciting as the day my daughter becomes a teenage girl who actually feels okay about her body.

take my pets, please: I Turned on Our Animals as Soon as I Had a Baby

Melissa Anderson Sweazy

THREE FINE PETS TO A GOOD HOME!

Tigger aka the Kitten Fine Attributes include: Eating food off the dining room table, particularly in the sixty-second window it takes to get from the table to the kitchen for the baby's drink and back. He will time you. Running underfoot while you carry the baby downstairs. Usually preceded by a banzai cry to give you a sporting chance. Crying until you personally escort him to his dinner, and then crying until you pet him as he eats. It's kind of like breast-feeding, except with zero benefits.

The Donkey aka Murphy Loves to bark while your child attempts to nap. Loves to bark while you attempt to nap. "Accidentally" runs over the baby while she's on the floor. Despite hundreds of dollars and countless hours spent on training, responds to commands only if he feels like it.

The Elder Statesman aka Andy Craps on the floor of your house, sometimes behind a potted plant. Sometimes in it. Usually just in plain view. Purrs.

This is the ad that I compose in my head, usually around 3:00 AM, when the Kitten scratches and yowls at our daughter's nursery door. The ad gets decidedly more violent around 5:30 AM, when both cats try to break down our door. In a blind rage, one of us stumbles over to the door and flings it open. The Kitten promptly knocks over the bedside water glass and the heavy book we use to block it from him. Crotchety, burly Andy (think Jack Palance with fur) picks a fight with the Border collie, he of the nervous skin condition. Andy hisses. Murphy scratches his belly, vibrating the entire bed frame. My husband growls at the pets to cut it out.

Too late.

From across the hall, the baby starts to wail. My husband threatens to kill them all. I tell him to back off, because I want to do the deed myself.

This used to be a love story. Through some combination of luck, good looks, and old-fashioned moxie, two cats and a puppy found their way into my home and my heart. I grew up with pets, so it was a fait accompli that I would cobble together a furry menagerie of my own. As annoying as they could be at times, they were mine. I had rescued each of them from an uncertain future in a shelter. There were the emergency operations for Andy, the labyrinthlike maze we set up so the Kitten could be outside, and for a brief, misguided period, the commercial agent for the devastatingly handsome Murphy. I had groomed them, fed them, cuddled with them, and kept them alive for most of my adult life. Naturally, I felt like this qualified me for parenthood. I could just see my child curling up with the kitty for an afternoon nap. She would ride around the living room astride the goofy, loyal collie. It would be a sweet, peaceful, animal–baby kingdom.

And then the kid came.

We had been warned that the pets would get the shaft once the baby became the focal point of our existence. What I was not prepared for was the depth of my hatred for beings I once claimed to love, and how quickly the switch happened.

The dog, our former "baby," was simply an inconvenient mass of baby-slicing claws and potential allergens. The cats left hair balls like a bread-crumb trail for the baby to follow. When not literally underfoot, they lay about on the baby's things. They yowled outside every closed door. The hair. The ever-present hair that no amount of vacuuming could banish. When we had a precious, spare moment to ourselves, elderly Andy would defecate on the carpet, and sometimes someone would eat said feces and lick the baby.

And the kicker? They loved the baby. We couldn't use pet jealousy or aggression toward her to justify our feelings, and that just made us hate them even more.

But, for the sake of the family, we tried to make it work. My husband, the hero (already laboring under massive sleep deprivation while we co-slept), rose extra early to take the dog on the long walks to which he was accustomed. We stepped up doggie "day care" to twice a week to help him burn off all

"... we raced each other inside the house, scooping up our pets and whispering our gratitude into their fur. We had hated them but, as it turned out, not enough."

that pent-up energy. The cats were nuzzled and lavished with treats when not trying to trip me on the way down the stairs with the baby.

"Why don't you just get rid of them?" a friend asked after listening to my rant. She matter-of-factly announced that she'd given away her cats shortly after having her baby. She placed an ad in Craigslist, interviewed a few candidates, and poof! No more cat hair to fish out of the baby's mouth. I left in a funk of confusion and jealousy. That was actually an option?

Getting rid of them was what those other people did. Before we found Murphy, I spent hours volunteering at animal rescue groups and trolling online shelter sites in my search for the One, shaking my head at those lazy, callous people who had dumped their pets because they no longer had time. They had made a commitment to these animals, and surely a little sleep deprivation and maddening annoyance couldn't justify breaking such a promise, right?

Still, the hatred gnawed a hole in me. I was heartened to hear from my friend Lisa, who confessed to lying awake at night, imagining braining her incessantly barking dogs. She admitted that she was horrified by the disturbing, violent images, insisting that she used not to be "that kind of person." And then she realized, she wasn't that person. She was just someone trying to get sleep.

Sleep deprivation was definitely taking its toll: on me, my husband, our family. If the family unit wasn't functioning, it was our obligation to fix it. But did this mean cutting out a portion of the family to restore some sanity? Signs pointed to yes.

Then there was the Colorado incident.

We left town for Christmas vacation, leaving the pets in the care of our beloved sitter. I called on New Year's Eve, letting her know we would be extending our trip an extra day. She called back, frantic. She didn't have our trip on the books. In a perfect storm of misunderstanding and double-bookings, she hadn't been to the house. For an entire week.

We waited in tense, agonizing silence for her to report back as she raced to the house. Dread knotted up my stomach. *Please, please be okay,* I prayed. Amazingly, they were. They drank out of the toilet and noshed on the giant bag of cat food one of them managed to tip over. They even had the courtesy to pick one carpet to use as their restroom. Not another piece of furniture was touched. They happily received the pet sitter when she arrived to check on them, accepting walks and love and belly rubs, and then resumed lounging around the house like nothing had happened.

I hung up with the sitter, and my husband and I sat down on the floor and sobbed. When we got home, we raced each other inside the house, scooping up our pets and whispering our gratitude into their fur. We had hated them but, as it turned out, not enough.

I now understand and respect the decision any parent makes to relocate their pets. No amount of bellowing from animal advocacy groups can convince me that an animal should take precedence over a child—or a parent's ability to take care of that child. But we will be keeping ours—the feces eater, the ambusher, and the bully. It turns out the baby loves them, and sometimes we do, too.

a private matter: Sorry,
Sexperts—In Our House, It's a Vajayjay

Jeanne Sager

My daughter stood up from the potty and reached down.
I thought she was scratching. But then I realized she was trying
to shake herself off—just like Daddy!

I'd been dreading this moment, from the moment in the
delivery room when my ob-gyn announced this was one less cir-
cumcision he'd have to perform—his way of telling us we had a
new baby girl.

It was time to tell Jillian about girls and boys. The job was
apparently firmly in my hands—by virtue of our common geni-
talia. My husband—who'd inadvertently caused all this, I should
point out—was conveniently playing the gender card.

So, I waded in.

"Honey, you don't have to shake, you know," I told her.
"Girls just wipe."

I earned an exasperated two-year-old eye roll.

"I wee'd," she told me. "Have to get it off me. Daddy does it."

Indeed, he does. And to get the potty-training ball rolling, we'd spent hours proving that Mommy and Daddy use the potty. Now that we've gotten her good and convinced—and she's of the mind that she belongs in the bathroom even if the door is closed—we're paying for it.

At least I am.

I sighed. "Yes, Daddy does it. Daddy's a boy. You're a girl like Mommy. You don't have to shake."

She shook her head. She stomped. What did I know? I'm the mom. She's the expert.

"Noooo," she said. "You're not a girl. You're Mommy."

Talk about kicking an old broad when she's down. I did my own eye roll and changed the subject. Man, that was a close one.

I'm not ready for this talk. It's not the sexual connotations that creep me out—I prefer to think of my daughter as an asexual being, not unlike her grandparents (who were blessed, by the way, with two miracles of Biblical proportions—me and my brother). It's putting the words out there.

I don't say "vagina." I don't even say "breasts." "Breast-feeding" is acceptable because the emphasis is on the latter syllables. It starts out kind of gross and ends kind of nice. Otherwise, they're "cleavicles." Or "cleavlage." Or "breastesses."

Call me too immature to have given birth. But vaginas give me the willies. And penises make me giggle.

They're not even sexy words. I can picture the teacher from *Ferris Bueller* standing at the front of a class saying, "Bueller?

"... I'm facing the fact that something I just don't like to talk about will soon be a big topic of conversation."

Anyone? Bueller?" then turning to the blackboard with his glasses perched on the end of his nose and announcing in that awful, grating voice, "Today we are going to learn about vaginas."

See? Not sexy. And not my kind of language.

I'm with Oprah. It's a "vajayjay." Or that chick from *Scrubs*, the one who always says "frick"? She calls it a "bajango." I like that. It sounds like something I'd have on my body, a piece of the anatomy that belongs on the same person who has watermelon slices painted on her toenails.

Even when the pain of pushing got so intense that I didn't care who walked into the delivery room (as long as they were there to get that thing out of there), I wasn't ready to talk vaginas. While I muttered obscenities under my breath, I had one thought going round and round my head: "My cha-cha hurts."

So, no, I'm not ready for this talk.

The experts tell you to be "direct and matter-of-fact" when you're laying out the gender line for your kids. In fact, the psychologist over at Babycenter.com says, "Follow the rule of thumb: 'Is this how I would tell her about elbows or knees?' Give her the anatomically correct name for the body part ('vagina,' 'penis').

"Using funny or silly words," she says, "will just confuse her and, if anything, makes the discussion a bigger deal."

But we're not talking about the elbows or the knees. Who has funny or silly words for their elbow? Who uses their elbow for . . . well, you know?

Okay, so I said it wasn't about the sexual creepiness. But the "funny" words we all use had to come from somewhere. And since I haven't met many people who admit to talking about "penises" in the bedroom (or "vaginas" for that matter), I'm going to go out on a limb and tell you the two connect.

I learned about sex the old-fashioned way—on the school bus. And no one dared give names to the "privates," which were most often referred to as "down there" by a burly classmate whose voice still cracked into a giggle while he was trying to guffaw.

But as an adult, not big on the diagrams in the gynecologist's office—and not that big on the gyno's office to begin with—I'm facing the fact that something I just don't like to talk about will soon be a big topic of conversation.

And I'm scared. There. I've said it. Call me a bad mommy, but I can't picture myself going the clinical route. I'm a talker. I'm an explainer. Short, sweet, and direct just is not my way. I can't imagine I'm alone. A Gallup poll showed that 67 percent of parents use actual names to refer to male and female body parts. So, what about the other 33 percent of us?

Are we prudes? Apparently we've made it to parenthood, so I kind of doubt it.

Some might think they're avoiding a very embarrassing conversation in the middle of the supermarket down the road. I don't envy them the day their kids learn to sound out *T-r-o-j-a-n* at the pharmacy counter.

I'm sure some of the other parents are scared of the sex talk with a two-year-old. I know I would be.

But Jillian isn't concerned about sex, and neither am I. I'm not even afraid of what she'll say outside the house. She's been told very honestly that, after she "wees," she needs to wipe lest she develop crotch rot. And she's used the words *crotch* and *rot* together in public.

I'm just not a vagina kind of girl.

So, when she gets around to asking, I'll be honest—the way I know how. "You and Mommy have a cha-cha," I'll tell her. "Go ask Daddy what he has."

fight club: I Argue with My Wife in Front of Our Kids

Darren Taffinder

The other day, my wife and I had a huge fight over money.
Apparently, I'm a tightfisted miser who is obsessed with checking our joint account (online banking has a lot to answer for).
My wife, on the other hand, is an out-of-control shopaholic
intent on driving us into the nearest homeless shelter. Three
of George Carlin's seven dirty words were used, anatomically
impossible head placements were suggested, and several alter-
natives to birth control were proposed—all in front of our
eleven-year-old daughter.

An hour later, after I'd stormed off and come crawling back,
the guilt started to set in. Had we psychologically damaged our
daughter for life? After all, when it comes to arguing, isn't the
cardinal rule: not in front of the kids?

Whenever I think of parental blowouts, I always think of my fifth birthday, when my parents had their famous "birthday cake" argument. My wannabe Martha Stewart mother had baked me a huge soccer-themed cake, complete with players, two goals, spectators, and even a scoreboard. It was spectacular.

What happened next is still clouded with controversy, even after thirty-one years.

After my birthday party, about half of the cake was left. According to my mother, my dad was instructed to take it to Granny's, share a few slices of it with her and my extended family, and then bring the rest of it back. My dad contends that he was told specifically to let them have the rest of the cake. The one undisputed detail is that my dad returned without the cake. To put it mildly, my mother got a little upset. Tempers were lost, followed by one of those epic full-on screaming matches that seem less like an argument and more like a clash of civilizations. My dad spent a rather uncomfortable night on the sofa. My reaction to losing my birthday cake is not remembered.

My parents, on the whole, have always been a happy couple. I didn't grow up in a house full of constant resentment and sniping. Plates were not broken on the kitchen floor. There were no court-imposed anger management classes. But, on occasion, they liked to have a good old row.

Like everything in parenting, when it comes to fighting, you're damned if you do and certainly damned if you don't. My brother-in-law's parents never argued in front of him while he was growing up. In fact, he has never seen them utter a cross word to each other in his entire life. As a result, rather than seeing squabbles as part of a healthy relationship, he saw them as a sign of doom. He broke up with several girlfriends during his twenties just because they had an argument.

I'm not suggesting you should pull up chairs so that your children can have front-row seats to your fights. Nor am I suggesting that all arguments are positive life experiences. A few years ago, a friend and her ex had an argument in front of their six-year-old son during which the ex threatened to punch her. Not a great male role model there.

"When it comes to arguing, you can't always wait until the kids are asleep."

What I am saying is that we all need to relax a little. We have become so anxious about the negative impacts our actions have on the kids that we have lost our sense of balance. Our children's psyches are not delicate spiderwebs. They are actually much sturdier than we give them credit for. Though, like every adult, I question a number of Mom and Dad's dubious parenting decisions ("Oh, he'll grow out of it" isn't a great strategy for dealing with dyslexia), I don't think their arguing had a negative effect on me. I was too busy playing with my *Star Wars* figures and, as I got older, trying to summon the courage to talk to girls to take much notice of their arguments. And when it comes to arguing, you can't always wait until the kids are asleep. That's a recipe for simmering resentment.

Just as too much arguing is a sign of a bad relationship, so is too little. My wife and I are about average on the arguing bell curve. We both have our moments, and I think it's good for our daughter to see all sides of a relationship. Sometimes we pick fights with each other just to clear the air. In many ways, a good fight is like a violent summer storm, and it's a great way to relieve the tensions that build up in our daily lives. Life is stressful, and, sometimes, we all need to release our inner Hulk.

What did our daughter think of our blowout? Did we psychologically damage her for life? Well, it's probably too early to tell, but I don't think she's going to need long-term counseling. She's seen us argue before, and she knew that we weren't going to get divorced or separated. She was, dare I say it, happy—more money for the swear box! At the end, my wife and I both apologized to each other. I think that's the best lesson. No matter what you say in the heat of the moment, afterward there is always a "sorry," and that's definitely good for our children to witness.

full house: What's So Wrong with Wanting Six Kids?

Katie Allison Granju

I always knew I wanted a large family. As a little girl, I read and reread *Cheaper by the Dozen,* and I loved watching *The Brady Bunch* and *Eight Is Enough.* My own family of origin had only three children, but my mother said more than a few times over the years that she wished she had given birth to at least one more. It didn't matter, though, because our slightly dilapidated old farmhouse often seemed to contain more children than just our three. We had plenty of cousins, neighbors, and friends hanging around, and my happiest memories are of our house full of people, music, laughter, and food.

I married young, before most of my peers, and by age thirty I had three children. Despite the fact that larger families were rather out of vogue, and despite being the subject of criticism and ridicule among many of my socially conscious set, I wished for more children. But, with some trepidation, we took steps to make sure there would be no more babies. This decision made sense logically; I secretly feared our marriage ultimately wouldn't make it, and single parenthood is hard enough with even one child. In my heart, however, I continued to long for a larger "bunch." I felt in some primal way that my family wasn't quite complete.

I found myself sidling up to the mothers I'd occasionally meet at the park, at La Leche League meetings, or at my kids' schools—mothers with four, five, and six children—and asking about their lives. Were they happy? Did they ever feel overwhelmed? In fact, I found that these mothers-by-choice of large gaggles of children were some of the most serene, self-actualized people I knew. Their lives had a clear "center," and it gave them a sense of direction—a North Star, if you will.

But in a culture where approximately 2.1 children-per-mama is the statistical norm, even my three children—born in fairly rapid succession over only six years—stirred some comment. "Don't you two know what causes that yet?" people would ask me and my husband. Even with three, we had to buy a "big family" vehicle—the dreaded minivan—and we no longer fit in restaurant booths for four.

And then my marriage *did* end. For several years, I was single, sharing the parenting of my three growing children across two households with my ex-husband. I figured I might marry again, but I assumed that if I ever did, the man in question would certainly say that three was plenty.

I was wrong. The man I married told me he not only loved my three but wanted them to have more siblings. I was thrilled.

And today we are the HickJu Bunch, as we jokingly tell people (his name is Hickman, mine is Granju). After giving birth to my youngest child, eleven months after our wedding day, we had four children between us, and we hope to have a fifth. While it's pretty unlikely, even a sixth child isn't completely outside the realm of possibility for us.

When I tell people I have four children, and that I would like to have more, the most common response is one of—for lack of a better word—distaste. "I would never want to do that," women say to me. And you know what? As a strongly pro-choice woman, I am extremely pleased that we live in a culture where what women want has become the primary factor in whether they have five children, one child . . . or no children at all. There is no question that raising a passel of kids is time-consuming and expensive, and requires a certain tolerance for chaos. I freely admit that it isn't for everyone, and I'd never suggest that anyone take on the role unless it's something she really, really wants.

Historically, large families were literally foisted onto women. Pushy husbands, religious or cultural expectations, and lack of access to birth control conspired to knock up women—again and again and again. Today, however, most American women who become mothers to a brood are making a conscious choice. And it's a choice that is worthy of the same respect given to those who choose to have one child, or no children at all.

But I will tell you from personal experience that it is not always afforded that kind of respect. While we do appear to have a pop culture fascination with big families—witness the interest in the Duggars, *Jon and Kate Plus 8,* and even the Jolie-Pitt

"... we had to buy a 'big family' vehicle— the dreaded minivan— and we no longer fit in restaurant booths for four."

brood—our focus is somewhat akin to the way one would observe a circus sideshow act, complete with requisite smug ridicule. In fact, many people I know personally, who make it a point to actively support reproductive rights, don't seem to believe that those rights should also extend to actual reproduction; this is especially true for pro-choice folks, who seem to believe I am committing some kind of heinous eco-crime by giving birth.

There's no question that a bigger family potentially has a larger environmental impact. For me to deny this would be intellectually dishonest. However, it's simplistic to suggest that everyone having tiny families—or even zero population growth— would offer the answer to all the world's woes. And until the earnest parents of a single child who lecture me about my family size start using cloth diapers (I do), or move from the car-centric burbs to an urban neighborhood that allows them to walk most places (I have), or join the local food co-op that supports sustainable, organic agriculture (I've belonged since college), well, I suggest they reconsider their holier-than-thou criticism.

Don't misunderstand: I am certainly not claiming any prize for exemplary green living, but I do notice that large families seem to be an easy target for criticism from individuals who should take a hard look at their own environmental footprints before worrying so much about mine. I believe that one of my primary responsibilities as the mother of all these children is to teach them to be conservationists in their own lives. And a large family—where people simply have to share, make do with less, and live with hand-me-downs—offers a perfect laboratory for imparting this mind-set.

Beyond worrying about the environment, critics of larger families also seem to focus on the idea that children with many siblings miss out on parental attention. I'm not sure this is such a bad thing. While children certainly need and thrive on appropriate levels of parental involvement and attention, our twenty-first-century American belief that the relationship with one's parents is the only family relationship that really matters to children is questionable. In today's smallish families, mothers and fathers alone are expected to be everything to their children: providers, nurturers, playmates, educators, and more.

In larger families—particularly larger families that are also lucky enough to have cousins, aunts, uncles, and grandparents in the mix—children get more attention from more people, all of whom love them and share a bond with them. I frequently tell my children, as my parents told me, that their brothers and sisters will be there for them long after I am gone; it's the relationship likely to last longer than any other one they have in their lives. This is a gift I feel proud to be offering my children, even if it does mean that I have less time for individual flash card drills.

Whether we remain a family with four kids or end up with one or two more, I am happy with my choice to become mama to many. That doesn't mean I don't have days when I am very tired, or days when I wish I had more money to spend on things like pedicures for me rather than another pair of soccer cleats. I sometimes wish I had more time to write and fewer loads of laundry to wash. And don't even get me started on what it's been like parenting my eldest through adolescence thus far.

Raising a bunch of kids is hard work. But it's the best, most satisfying work I've ever done. And for those of you who may be considering making the same choice—and it is a choice—I say go for it. Deciding to give birth to another baby is an exercise in optimism. Big families may be old-fashioned, but so are plenty of things that the modern world could use more of, like an abiding faith in the future. It's not crazy to embrace chaos for the sake of love.

suck city: I Hope My Child Never Gets Rid of That Pacifier

Pamela Appea

During a recent appointment, the doctor said this was the summer for my son to give up his pacifier.

"Tell your son that he's a big boy now. There are other babies out there that need his pacifiers," the doctor said, in a kind but no-nonsense tone.

I nodded.

"We'll do our best," I said with a bright smile.

I was lying through my teeth. The pacifier fairy will not be coming to our apartment this summer, or for as long as I can help it.

This puts me in the minority on my playground, where I constantly hear other mothers bragging to each other: "Oh, my daughter never used a pacifier," and, "Well, my son had his

Binky two, three months tops, and then we took it away. And he's perfectly fine without one."

My son is almost two and has loved his pacifier ever since a nurse at our hospital gave him one in the NICU, where he spent two weeks after being born prematurely. As soon as he left the hospital, he graduated to his second pacifier, a Nuk butterfly model that seemed to take up most of his face. I can't count how much money I've spent on pacifiers since, but to me it's money well spent.

Since he was born, my son's pacifiers have served as a way for me to get him to sleep sooner rather than later. They have helped him calm down during New York City subway rides and during rough transitions from home to day care when he's tired. The pacifier nips a kicking, crying, screaming, toddler temper tantrum right in the bud. And my son automatically reaches for his pacifier when he needs something more than a book to look at or some milk to drink or a playmate to hug. Why are people so eager to give up such a magic bullet?

It would make sense if there were strong scientific evidence that the pacifier was truly evil. But it doesn't seem *so* bad.

The World Health Organization and the United Nations Children's Fund issued a statement that strongly discouraged pacifier use "because of [the] perceived interference with breast-feeding." But other studies have found that once breast-feeding is established, pacifiers are helpful for babies who crave nonnutritive sucking. And in a 2001 *Journal of the American Medical Association* study, the conclusion was "that pacifier use is a marker of breast-feeding difficulties or reduced motivation to breast-feed, rather than a true cause of early weaning." So, in plain English, the pacifier didn't cause the breast-feeding to stop. Moms who were going to stop breast-feeding anyway, due to work or difficulties or other reasons, elected to use a pacifier as a transition.

"Thanks to that little object, I've gotten more sleep . . . and less stress."

There have been a scattered number of reports that pacifier use is connected with ear infections among babies. The *British Journal of Community Nursing* did a 2002 study on ear infections and pacifier use. It would be inaccurate to say the study was *pro-*pacifier, but one line jumped out at me: "Rather than advising a parent not to use a pacifier for fear of causing otitis media [otherwise known as ear infection], advice in relation to this issue might best be restricted to pacifier users suffering from the problem in order to reduce the chances of recurrence." So, the Brits say, if you think your baby is suffering from ear infections because of pacifier use, then stop. But if your baby is not having ear infections, then . . . don't? Will do!

As for the alleged damage pacifiers cause to baby teeth, even the American Academy of Pediatric Dentistry doesn't seem concerned. They say: "Most children stop sucking on thumbs, pacifiers, or other objects on their own between two and four years of age. No harm is done to their teeth or jaws." The stricter American Dental Association recommends that children cut out their pacifier by age two. But, at the same time, an article for the *Journal of the American Dental Association* states that pacifiers are preferable to giving older babies and toddlers nighttime bottles of milk or juice. The article also goes on to say that "teething babies might find relief by using a pacifier." Booyah!

My enthusiasm for studies like these (you should have seen my glee when the American Academy of Pediatrics said pacifiers helped prevent SIDS!) indicate that I am clearly addicted to giving my son a pacifier. I confess it. Thanks to that little object, I've gotten more sleep (still not enough) and less stress. I've read a lot of books, never skipped a shower, and been able to take my pacified son to nice restaurants.

Now that he is in day care, my son doesn't want his pacifier as much as before. He loves playing for hours and can't seem to run while keeping the pacifier in his mouth. When he wants to talk, he has to take his pacifier out to be understood.

Just today, in the morning rush to his day care, as he was running out the door, my son dropped the chain that holds his blue pacifier. "Go get your pacifier. Don't forget it!" I said, sounding rather desperate. "You're going to need it."

He ran back and picked it up. Then he changed his mind. He turned around and handed it to me. His message was clear: *You need this more than I do.*

the not-so-happy accident: I Wasn't Totally Happy to Turn Up Pregnant a Third Time

Keri Fisher

"I hate to be the one to lay something so heavy on you," the ultrasound technician began, "but it looks like you're pregnant."

Pregnant? Impossible. I was on Depo-Provera, the wonder-drug injectable birth control you only have to take four times per year. No periods, no hassle. After a year on it, I was in love. Or rather, up until that moment I was.

I had had some minor bleeding the day before. "It sounds like nothing," my doctor had said. "But why don't you come in for an ultrasound and we'll take a look."

"This couldn't be an early miscarriage, could it?"

"Oh, no," she had assured me. "No birth control is 100 percent, but Depo is pretty close." How close? According to the Web site: 99.7 percent.

I lay on the table, shaking. Despite my earlier miscarriage question, I had never really considered the possibility I might be pregnant. Grapefruit-sized tumor, sure. Benign cyst? Possibly. But pregnant? On almost-one-hundred-percent-reliable Depo? Never.

I thought back to my initial miscarriage question. "Is there a heartbeat?"

"Yes, there's a heartbeat."

She sent me out to the waiting room so she could take measurements from the pictures, and I sat and wept alone as the other couple in the waiting room watched me nervously. They were pregnant. They probably assumed I was crying because I wasn't.

I was still shaking when I went back to see the nurse practitioner, who eyed me nervously and asked what I wanted to do. She knew nothing about me. I could've been unemployed and single. Pregnant from an extramarital fling.

I was none of those things. I was married, fairly young and fairly stable, and had two wonderful sons. I had no reason not to keep this baby—except, of course, that I didn't want it. I didn't say that, however. I just looked at her evenly and said, "I'm okay," even though I clearly wasn't.

Reassured, the nurse read from my file, "Well, it looks like you're seventeen weeks along. . . . "

Seventeen weeks. Four months. I was four months pregnant and hadn't known it. I was one of those women I always mocked when I read about them in tabloids.

The next few weeks were a slow blur. According to the measurements, I had received two Depo injections since conceiving the baby. No one knew what Depo could do to a fetus. I was referred to a specialist, who of course couldn't see me for two weeks because of the Christmas holiday. I felt frozen in time, fearing something was horribly wrong, and if it were, wondering if I'd ever be able to abort a four-and-a-half-month-old fetus.

I didn't have to worry. Ironically, Depo is about the best thing you can be on while pregnant. It's pure progesterone, which is often given to pregnant women to help maintain a pregnancy. My ultrasound looked good, the fetus was exactly where it ought to be, and it was a girl. After my younger son, Ronan, was born, I had resigned myself to life without pigtails and prom dresses. But there she was.

Everyone was thrilled. When I got home from that first ultrasound, crying to my sister, her husband wanted to go out and celebrate. My mom cried happily on the phone. My husband, unflappable as ever, smiled and hugged me. A pregnancy is wonderful news, so joyous. But I had fought this. I had taken great pains to prevent this. And that didn't seem to matter.

When everyone around you is happy about your pregnancy, it's hard not to get caught up in it as well. I wanted to be happy. It seemed silly and shortsighted to think about how close I had been to being done with babies. This summer, my boys were going to be in camp full-time. I had been looking forward to my freedom. With every milestone Ronan crossed, I had felt excited rather than sad. No more nursing? Hooray! Done with the high chair? Good riddance! Sayonara, crib! See you later, sippy cup!

I wasn't a nostalgic mom. I'm not a nostalgic person. I don't know exactly when Ronan stopped nursing (around eleven months?) or when he started walking (fourteen months? maybe fifteen?); all I know is that he and I have shared this forward momentum, this movement toward independence for both of us.

"I had no reason not to keep this baby—except, of course, that I didn't want it."

During the entirety of Ronan's first year of life, my sister would ask me, "Don't you want another? Just a little bit?" (She has five kids and clearly didn't want to be alone in her insanity.) But I was certain. No doubts. Two was perfect. There were two of them and two of us. It seemed fair, equitable. We could fit in a booth at a restaurant. Heck, we could go to a restaurant. Two was the right amount.

Except now it wasn't. Now, we'd have three kids.

For a long time, I couldn't bring myself to admit my doubts, my fears. Two of my closest friends were struggling with fertility, and here I was, unable not to get pregnant. I was embarrassed by my lack of excitement, by my inner unhappiness. I was sure that no one wanted to hear it: I wasn't a teenager; I wasn't living in poverty; I was a thirty-five-year-old woman in a loving marriage with two great kids and a supportive husband. I was the poster child for pregnancy.

So, I played along. I laughed with everyone about the bizarre unlikelihood of it all, about how it was possible I hadn't known for so long, about this miracle child, who so clearly wanted to be here. And I tried to want her to be here.

When I finally admitted to my husband that I was stressed and anxious and scared about this child, he was calm and reassuring without being patronizing. The more I talked about it, the more I found out that I wasn't alone. Friends of mine who had actually planned their pregnancies admitted to experiencing doubt and hesitation. No one thought any less of me when I confessed my true feelings.

And as the pregnancy has progressed, I have felt moments of excitement and anticipation, pure wonder at the tiny person growing inside of me. When I saw her perfect little face on my second ultrasound, I cried again, but this time they were tears of joy. I have found myself on more than one occasion trolling the aisles at Nordstrom Rack, fingering tiny designer dresses with matching bloomers. Two friends recently gave birth to girls, and as I watched them sleep through our coffee dates, I thought to myself: I can do this. Just because I didn't want to doesn't mean I won't be able to.

I know that when she gets here, I'll fall in love and wonder how my life was complete before her. I'll breathe in her scent as she falls asleep beside me and wonder how I ever could have doubted.

Pregnancies can be unwanted. But babies rarely are.

the little man: I Wanted
a Girl, but I Got a Boy—and How

Ondine Galsworth

My son's name was Ava in utero, until twenty-four weeks.
Everyone said it was a girl: the ultrasound technician, the psychic, and the prenatal yoga teacher. I was ecstatic about having a girl. It's what the baby's father and I both wanted—sweet Ava, our delicate flower.

Then the amnio gave us the real news: no genetic defects, a healthy son.

I was in the frozen foods section in the supermarket when I got the news. I called my baby's father immediately, sobbing hysterically, feeling guilty that I wasn't just relieved that my fetus was all right. "He's healthy, he's fine, but our daughter is a he!" Now we were both crying—mostly from relief and confusion and all those crazy emotions that come with the first months of pregnancy, waiting to see if everything is okay, but also in mourning for the daughter we had thought we were having.

"Boys are different: tornadoes of dirt, aggression, and passion."

Perhaps to punish us for naming him Ava as a zygote, my son, Boone, was born about as dainty as the Marlboro Man. The nurse said he had the neck strength of a three-week-old. Right away, when infants are only supposed to have a little bit in the bottle, he pounded down six ounces at a time like it was a Coors Light. He never spit up. He was an eating machine. Instead of losing weight the first week, like most babies, he gained a pound. At two months, the babysitter started calling him the man-baby.

Now, at a year and a half, he gets what I call his "work face" as he takes the filter out of the vacuum, empties it into the garbage, puts it back, replaces the cover, and then proceeds to vacuum. I say, "I get it, you are a boy."

But he continues to reassert his masculinity. He's like an advertisement for maleness, sort of like a peacock, except at this stage of the game he displays his testosterone by running at top speed into furniture, swan-diving off the table, and getting a bloody lip every other day. In fact, he is so covered in scrapes and bruises, I had to ask the doctor not to call Child Protective Services. I explained that I do not beat my child; he just falls his way through the day. She commented, "Wow, he really is beat up, but he's high energy. It's what boys do."

Boys also, apparently, yell. Shortly after my son's first birthday, he came up with a new sound—screaming bloody murder at the top of his lungs. Its loudness can only be compared to sounds heard outside of the city—like, say, the Serengeti, where fearsome fanged creatures bellow and then tear into the soft, warm underbelly of an impala.

There's shaking and roaring and hurling of objects, followed by a burning hate in his eyes as I pry him away from any dangerous electrical equipment. He stands in the hall, looking quite fierce in just a diaper, hands clenched into fists, elbows out, legs in half a squat. He's got the whole silverback gorilla thing down pat. After surveying the territory, avoiding any eye contact with me, he lifts up his arms, tilts his head back, and roars: "Grrrrrrr-rrrrrrrrrrrrrrrrrrrrrrrr!"

And, yes, it's kind of scary. The sound is deep and manly and menacing. It never ceases to surprise me when my cuddly, *Dora the Explorer*-loving, teddy bear–hugging, Goldfish cracker-eating toddler turns into the Incredible Hulk. We, his bumbling and inexperienced parents, have been wondering what the hell happened to our sweet child, now the maddest baby in New Jersey.

He just gets so puffed up and indignant at the lack of cooperation the WetVac is giving him. He'll drag it across the room toward me, hand me the hose, and make a deep, throaty sound as if to say, "Make this work, Mommy, or I'll go postal." He hates when things don't work. He curses in baby language, and like many men when they're trying to fix things around the house and can't, he kicks the object in question as if to punish it.

Baffled, his father and I kiss him, hug him, and give him organic sweet potatoes. We theorize on the cause of this angry sound: He's teething. He has to poop. He's thirsty. He's starving to death. He swallowed a guitar pick. It's the mosquito bites. Or maybe he just hates our guts.

This may sound ridiculous, but, before I had a child, I honestly always believed that if you treated children the same, their behavior would not indicate their sex. Even though most of my friends had children way before I did, and all of them said that boys behaved differently from girls, I still thought it was sexist to expect a major difference between little girls and little boys.

But, now—especially after yesterday's music class, when all the other kids were sitting in a circle playing with their maracas and tambourines, and my son stampeded up and down the room like King Kong until he belly-slid into the wall—I'm a believer. Boys are different: tornadoes of dirt, aggression, and passion. Girls are okay, I guess. Boone seems to like them. He kisses them every day while in child care at the gym, where he's known as "Ladies' Man."

Being a boy is hard on him sometimes. The fits of frustration can go on for hours, until he's throwing himself at my feet, defeated and whimpering. He's lost a battle. What battle, I'm not sure, but now he's sad, beaten, walking around flapping his arms like Woody Allen. "What's wrong, little man?" I ask my exasperated son. I get on my knees so I am down to my young primate's eye level and, channeling Jane Goodall, study his behavior more closely. From the kitchen floor, I observe his little shoulders going up around his ears. He lets out a sigh as if to say, "Man, this king of jungle stuff is hard!"

I can't believe I ever didn't want a boy. Like any mother, I just love everything about my baby, including his sex.

sisterhood, schmisterhood:

Those First Few Months, I Wanted to Talk to Anyone but Other New Moms

Kim Brooks

During the first few months of my son's life—the sleepless, harried months when every item of clothing I owned was caked with spit-up, when my boobs were like leaky spigots and my mind a brain-shaped glob of mud, when the phrase "sleeps like a baby" was as angrily suspect as creationism, those months that I've now come to think of as the dark ages of new-momhood—there was a refrain of advice from nearly everyone who witnessed my daily struggle to stay sane. "Go to a new-moms' group," they'd say.

The wisdom went: meeting regularly with other women experiencing the same major life-transition was the best thing I could do for myself and for my baby. These groups, everyone insisted, were indispensable when it came to both emotional support and networking, to making other mom friends and setting up future playgroups, not to mention putting my new baby on the road to socialization and a happy, well-adjusted life.

Still, I resisted. Did I really want to spend my precious few free moments schlepping the baby through the snow to some stranger's apartment? Wouldn't I rather spend them trying to get some work done, walking off my cantaloupe-size pregnancy pouch (when had I become a marsupial?), or, if I were to give in to my baser instincts, showering?

"Exactly," said a friend who had been in the same boat thirty years ago, when mothers' groups and women's groups of every variety were in their heyday. "This is exactly why women need new-moms' groups—so you can have people to bitch to about how hard it is." Bitching being one of my favorite pastimes, I was intrigued. Besides, I thought, what was the alternative: spending the rest of the winter marooned in my apartment without adult stimulation, perfecting my burping technique?

The first group I found by accident. I met a woman in a coffee shop with a baby girl a few weeks younger than my son. I was trying to pay for my decaf, soothe my ever-wailing child, and steer the seven-hundred-dollar stroller I'd splurged on, which apparently required extensive NASA training to maneuver. She was sitting calmly in a corner but had that "Help me: I haven't slept in seven weeks" look in her eyes. We started chatting. She mentioned that she hosted a group of new moms from her yoga studio. The next thing I knew, I was instructing little Roscoe about how to play nice with the other infants. But it wasn't he who needed instructing.

The other new moms were amazingly sweet, amazingly welcoming, and amazingly able to maintain a three-hour conversation on the benefits and disadvantages of soy formula. I participated enthusiastically in this discussion, just as, once, I had participated enthusiastically in discussions of the politics of the Middle East or the impact of global warming. Then I drove home in a stupor, feeling as though I'd spent the afternoon watching soap operas and eating Twinkies. The next group wasn't much better. Nor the next. At that point, I'd spent fifty-something dollars on pastries and Perrier. I'd learned more than I had ever wanted to learn about cradle cap and sex after episiotomies and breast pumps and nanny background-check services.

My breaking point occurred one drizzly afternoon, when the baby and I were on our way to a group. Instead of heading to the host's apartment, I found myself driving to my favorite bar, enjoying a glass of wine and a few minutes of reading with Roscoe snoozing in his stroller. There was a gay couple at a nearby table discussing Dennis Kucinich's candidacy, a woman sitting by herself at another table reading *Death in Venice*. Not a single word about bouncers or strollers or acid reflux or vaccinations or nipple soreness. It was beautiful—like listening to the ocean at night.

At that moment, I realized two things: First, I realized that new moms kind of suck. People generally aren't at their sharpest and most engaging when they're getting twenty minutes of sleep each night. Also, they're usually so busy trying to figure out how to survive the day, they don't have much energy left to contemplate, much less discuss, the world beyond the cradle.

"I realized that new moms kind of suck."

The second thing I learned was this: Just because two people are both new moms, that doesn't mean they'll necessarily have anything else in common. What I needed most of all in those early months was to be around people whose company I enjoyed, regardless of their parental status—people who would talk to me about the things I used to talk about, who would help me remember that in addition to being a new mother, I was still myself.

I ordered another glass of wine and resolved to call up a single, childless friend that night to let her regale me with tales of hook-ups and art-show openings and spontaneous weekend getaways. Perhaps Roscoe wouldn't enjoy it quite as much as drooling on other babies' toys while I discussed his sleep cycles and digestion. Then again, some of my earliest memories involve feeling bored and exasperated with the confines of little-kid-intended activities. I was the sort of obnoxiously precocious kid who preferred Stanley Kubrick to Disney, California rolls to chicken fingers. Maybe Roscoe felt the same way. Maybe he thought, in his little baby way, that one new mom was more than enough.

driven to it: I Breast-Fed in a Moving Vehicle

Vicki Glembocki

I'm going to get arrested.

My brain chants this, over and over, as I sit in the backseat of my minivan, next to the car seat where my two-month-old daughter, Blair, is supposed to be, all strapped in and safe. But she is not. She is, instead, lying across my lap. My tank top is pulled up, my left boob is hanging out, and Blair is latched on. None of this would be a problem, except for one thing. My mother is in the front seat, driving the car.

Oddly, less than two hours ago, I thought Blair and I were having a good day. I actually said this out loud to my husband, talking to him on my cell as Blair and I drove to the Philadelphia airport to pick up my mother, who was flying in to help out for a week.

"We're having a good day," I said.

"You are?" he answered, clearly surprised. This was the first official "good day" we'd had since Blair was born. The jaundice, the colic and the relentless crying, the two minutes of sleep, the impulse to kill the dog and anything else that made noise, and the madness of figuring out how to breast-feed another human being (who just, kind of, appeared) had all left me feeling entirely out of control.

But, today? Blair woke up from a nap at 2 PM, giving me precisely enough time to nurse her, get us both in the minivan, drive to the airport, pick up my mother, and drive back home before she'd need to nurse again at five. All was going well. Until, on the way home, I missed the exit. And we ended up in rush-hour traffic. Crawling. On a four-lane highway. With no way to pull over. For two-and-a-half hours . . . so far.

For the past hour of it, Blair has been screaming.

My mother is in the seat next to her, rocking the car seat, which isn't working. Neither is the air-conditioning I turned on full-blast to create a "shushing" sound. We both know she's hungry and that, because she's hungry, we're screwed.

I try not to look in the rearview mirror, where I can see Blair's face, all contorted into a massive black hole of a mouth, reflected in the mirror hanging on the headrest above her. My boobs are throbbing but not as much as my temples are. From that sound. That yelping, alien baby sound.

"Mom," I say, as if this is a sudden, new idea, and not something that I've been trying to grow the cojones to do for the past hour. "Mom, I am going to put the car in park. You are going to crawl up to the driver's seat and take over."

"Vicki, I can't drive in this . . . " she starts to say. But I've already opened my door and am trotting around the front of the minivan to the sliding door. In the amount of time it takes for me to get in and close the door, for my mother to stop saying, "Oh, my God. Oh, my GOD!" the traffic doesn't move an inch. I pull Blair out of her seat.

This is bad, I think, as I calculate the likelihood that the guy in the car next to us can see through the tinted windows, that this guy will dial 911, that 911 will call child services. Because this is illegal. I'm well aware of this. All states have mandatory child restraint laws for babies. This is very bad. I'm so going to jail.

Here's what I'm not aware of: If a cop pulls us over, I probably won't get arrested, just slapped with a $100 fine.

Here's what I'm also not aware of: Even though breast-feeding in public isn't illegal anywhere in the country, the guy in the car next to us could look over, see my boob, call 911, and claim I'm indecently exposing myself in public.

My friend in Seattle, Sarah, could have been fined for breaking the car seat law and cited with, say, obscenity when she followed her half-mile rule—as in, "a half-mile from home is okay." "When we were a few blocks from home," Sarah explains, "I'd sometimes give in, take my screaming son out of his seat, and let him nurse."

Luckily for Lisa, a woman I know in Ohio, that state and six others do give moms recourse, so she was perfectly safe when she was in the car and her three-month-old son was crying and her husband was "about to lose it" and she did "the hover": gymnastically positioning herself so she was half-lying over her son's infant seat so she could nurse him while he, and she, were still buckled in. "I was turned in such a way that I was staring out his window," Lisa says. "A female passenger in a neighboring car made eye contact with me and smiled."

"This is very bad. I'm so going to jail."

But all I can think about is what the cop will say when he pulls us over: "What if you got in an accident? What if something happened to the baby?" Which is why, as I slink down a little in the seat, I plot the baby-freaking-out defense I'll spout in response. "But, officer . . . she was *crying*."

In the front seat, I know my mother thinks that the fact that I'm making her drive the minivan during Philadelphia rush hour is a far worse offense than what I'm doing in the backseat. She knows nothing about what I'm going through. She didn't nurse me: her doctor instructed her not to. And, considering that old car seat she showed me last summer at a yard sale, the laundry basket with lace on the ends that was "exactly like the one we had for you," she also knows nothing about safely restraining children in moving vehicles.

"MOM!" I yell again, focusing entirely now on getting home, since Blair is nursing. And happy. And quiet. "Pull UP!"

I realize, then, that there is something about this experience that my mother and I have in common, something that crosses the generational boundary in this car. And it might have made me laugh, had I not still been squinting through the windows, on the lookout for Johnny Law. We both now know what it's like to be driving a car while your daughter screams at you from the backseat.

let them eat nuggets: My Kids Are Picky Eaters, and I'm Okay with That

Amy S. F. Lutz

I'll never forget an essay I read many years ago by a profes-sional foodie in which he described the highlight of both his parental and culinary careers: his young daughter, while dining with him in a restaurant, turned to him and said, "Daddy, this chicken tastes just like frog legs." I wish now I had noted the author's name, so I could track him down and chew him out for creating what I now understand was a wildly unrealistic set of expectations.

It was all so promising at the beginning. My oldest son, Jonah, was a wonderful eater when he was a baby. At one, it seemed there was nothing he didn't like: dim sum, asparagus, guacamole. Then he began to refuse things he had previously savored. My husband, Andy, and I joked about which foods had been "voted off the island" that week. After Jonah was diagnosed with autism, we assumed his extremely limited food preferences were part of his disorder. While it's true that many children on the autism spectrum have restricted diets, our next two children, both daughters, followed the same pattern of acceptance, then rejection, as they grew from babies into toddlers.

By the time my sister Keri, her husband, Matt, and their two young sons moved in with us a year and a half ago, I had fallen into the habit of feeding my children some permutation of chicken, macaroni and cheese, hot dogs, and fruit almost every night. Later, I would eat a late, grown-up dinner with Andy when he came home from work.

I wasn't proud of it. I never thought I'd be one of those moms who bought a little peace with overprocessed, unnaturally colored fare. But what were my options? Force the kids to eat the "adult" dinner I'd prepared? Send them to bed hungry? Neither choice particularly appealed to me. So, I consulted my pediatrician, who told us that the kids could meet many nutritional needs through fruit. And instead of dwelling on all the nitrates and refined flour my children were consuming, I focused on the critical protein and fat, which I had read were especially important for developing brains.

Still, I could guess what Keri and Matt, both chefs by training, thought of this diet: *not our boys.* I'm sure they assumed Declan and Ronan would be of the frog-legs-eating ilk—I certainly had. If ever children were bred to have broad palates, it's them. Their parents have a combined twenty years of restaurant experience. They make their own sushi, and they made their own baby food. When we go out to dinner, Matt can be counted on to order the most exotic dish on the menu, from sweetbreads to blood sausage to fried crickets.

"I never thought I'd be one of those moms who bought a little peace with over-processed, unnaturally colored fare."

And we felt their influence immediately. Our refrigerator was suddenly stocked with organic milk, yogurt, and eggs. We joined a farm cooperative in search of the best locally grown produce. We also started sitting down to dinner as a family. We gathered around the dining room table for braised oxtail, coq au vin, leg of lamb—and the fights I had so desperately tried to avoid. We read somewhere that children need to try new foods an average of nineteen times before they accept them, so we instituted a new rule: the kids had to take at least one taste of everything on their plates. One bite! It didn't seem that draconian to us. But every night there were tears: "I've had broccoli a million times, I already know I hate it!" "That smells disgusting!" "How big a bite?" "If I take a bite, can I have something else?" I freely admit that my six-year-old daughter, Erika, was often the instigator in these confrontations, but none of the kids—not even my culinarily advantaged nephews—embraced the risotto or the roasted parsnips. In the end, it always seemed to come down to a negotiation (okay, a bribe) for dessert.

That was eighteen months ago. Although we never sat down and explicitly talked about it, things have changed since then. Now, when Matt makes short ribs and noodles, the kids have noodles and hot dogs. Raw carrots, celery, and peppers—which the kids vastly prefer to cooked vegetables—are featured frequently on the menu. And our dinners are much more peaceful as a result. I know Keri has relaxed her standards with some reluctance, assuming her sons' palates would be greatly expanded were it not for their cousins' influence, but I'm not so sure. A recent article in the *New York Times* on picky eaters confirmed that children as a group are pickiest between the ages of two and five, and further explained that this phenomenon has its roots in evolutionary biology, as a defense mechanism to protect increasingly mobile toddlers from ingesting the countless new and potentially hazardous substances they encounter over the course of their daily explorations. And this makes sense to me.

After all, I know many kids who eat only chicken nuggets and macaroni and cheese. But I don't know one adult who does.

Not that we've completely given up. We still have our family dinners, and we set a positive example every day by exclaiming over the curried cauliflower, the turkey potpie, and the vegetable stir-fry that Matt and Keri prepare. We invite the kids to help with cooking projects of all kinds, from mixing pancake batter to shaping challah. Given how much effort and pleasure go into the preparation and consumption of food in our house, I think—I hope—it will be impossible for the kids to maintain their resistance for long.

screen queen: I Let My Toddler
Watch up to Six Hours of TV a Day

Jeanne Sager

I wake up to a remote control being bounced off the bridge of my nose. My daughter's voice has reached fever pitch, and it's only 6:30 in the morning. "Mom, Mom, can I watch TV? Please, please, please?" Now she's bouncing in the space recently vacated by my husband, who's off to work. Sure, it's early, but as far as I'm concerned, he's escaping. He doesn't have to listen to these piercing squeals.

If I give in, I won't have to either. I slip my hand out of the warmth of our comforter and slide it across flannel, feeling for the spot where the remote landed when it ricocheted from my nose. I point it in the general direction of the TV on our dresser and press *Power*. "There you go, honey," I mumble, but it's muffled, my head already burrowing back into my pillow.

My daughter goes from sixty to zero. Mommy's stint as a human trampoline is over. Jillian is already curled in a fetal position, her head on Daddy's pillow, her eyes fixed on Cookie Monster as he once again devours the letter of the day.

"Cookie Monster's funny," she says through a fit of giggles. Apparently, that joke never gets old. But I have.

Two years ago, I called my husband at work, horrified. My friend had dropped her three-year-old off for the day, and he'd spent the morning demanding the Disney Channel. "Can you believe it?" I asked Jonathan, full of righteous indignation. "I had books I picked up at the library yesterday. Boy books! Books just for him! And all he wants to do is watch TV. What are they teaching him?"

"It's okay, honey," he said. "Just let him watch a little TV. He's fine. I watched TV, and I'm fine, right?"

"Yeah, fine," I muttered to our then-infant daughter as I got off the phone. "Daddy's fine, but his world revolves around *SportsCenter*. And God forbid the cable goes out. . . . Oh, *nooooooooo.*"

I was darn sure my baby wasn't going to go down that road. I wasn't going to use TV as a babysitter. I wasn't going to park my kid in front of the idiot box. I wasn't going to be a cliché. And my position had some extra credibility, because I, *ahem,* didn't have television until I was seventeen. Yes, that's right, folks, step right up and see the '80s child who never even had the chance to figure out just what Willis *was* talking about.

When I was pregnant, I sported that fact like a badge of honor. The fact that I'd spent most of high school begging my parents for a cable hookup so I could get in on all the talk about Ross and Rachel was quickly forgotten.

"I love to read," I'd tell people, rubbing my belly. "And this one will, too. I'm going to limit how much TV little Squirmy watches. We're going to read books every night before bed, and every morning. You know, I didn't have TV, and I could sort my parents' mail when I was two and a half."

Jillian's two and a half now. She can't sort our mail.

She *can* tell you *Curious George* airs after *Sesame Street*. Then we switch the channel. What she watches next depends, really, on when I rouse myself from my cocoon and head downstairs for my morning caffeine injection. If it's time for *Pinky Dinky Doo*, the TV in the living room is tuned to NOGGIN while I putter in the kitchen. If *The Upside Down Show* is still on, I'm open to negotiations.

"*Cars* or *The Little Mermaid*?" I ask.

"How 'bout . . . um, this one?" Jillian counters, grabbing *Blue's Clues: Shapes and Colors* off her shelf at the bottom of our DVD collection.

I don't even blink. Whipping the disc out of the box, I do a quick switch in the DVD player, and she settles on the couch with a yogurt drink and plate of toast.

By the time she wanders down the hall to my office thirty minutes later, I've made three phone calls and answered a host of e-mails. I've checked in with my editor and scheduled two interviews—one face-to-face, one on the phone, set for fifteen minutes from now.

So, I couldn't be happier to see she's brought another movie with her. This time, it's *Thomas' Trusty Friends*, and she wants to watch it in the office. Not a problem—that's why there's a DVD/VCR combo sitting beside my printer and a TV on top of the shelving unit filled with coloring books and puzzles. It's looking like this might be one of those days when Jillian watches something like six hours of television.

Somewhere, the me of two years ago is holding her head in her hands. After all, the media reports will tell you kids shouldn't be watching television at all, let alone all day.

Television commercials—isn't this ironic—are aired daily with suggestions of outdoor activities to get your kids away from the tube. Mommy magazines are full of numbers from the American Academy of Pediatrics (AAP)—zero hours of television recommended for children under two, and all that. The AAP says, "Research has shown that children who consistently spend more than four hours per day watching TV are more likely to be overweight." Their experts say, "Kids who view violent events, such as a kidnapping or murder, are also more likely to believe that the world is scary and that something bad will happen to them." And, let's not forget, the AAP says, "Research also indicates that TV consistently reinforces gender-role and racial stereotypes."

So, let me get this straight: I'm raising a fat racist who's going to be afraid of everything, a girl who's going to fall all over herself to let men be the boss.

Tell that to the little girl playing in her toy kitchen in the next room. Her pants are falling off her skinny hips. Tonight, she's going to beg, as she does every other night, for repeated readings of her favorite bedtime story, *Georgie and the Noisy Ghost*.

When I finally get her to bed, she'll tell me she loves me. And when I say it back, she'll smile. "'Cause I'm the most beautiful, most smartest girl in the world. I'm smarter than Daddy and everybody."

Oh dear, what am I going to do about her self-esteem?

The truth is, I'm not crazy about all the TV watching in my house—whether it's Jillian or my husband in front of the screen.

"I wasn't going to use TV as a babysitter. I wasn't going to park my kid in front of the idiot box."

But I sacrifice to the TV gods in exchange for a work-from-home job, one that lets me spend more time with my daughter but requires me to offer her a smaller piece of my attention during the day.

It's not a day-care provider parking her in front of the screen; it's her mother, the same lady who curls up on the couch for a solid hour in the afternoon, reading *Make Way for Ducklings* and *Goodnight Moon*. It's the same woman who spends bath time giving voices to the rubber duckies and spelling with foam letters on the wall. It's her mother, who will kiss her good night and tell her she's the smartest and most beautiful girl in the world, and that, yes, she can watch *The Adventures of Elmo in Grouchland* in the morning.

to hell with baby-proofing:
I'm Not Securing Any Cabinets

Erin K. Blakeley

Our apartment is a baby booby trap. Between our ladder bookshelves, our tangled yards of electronic wiring, and our anti–feng shui decorating style, we are tripping over all the hazards the baby experts warn about.

But, instead of crawling through our apartment and barricading, battening down, or turning our living space into a giant bubble, we've come up with a novel solution. We've decided . . . not to.

Ten months ago, the notion that we would blow off baby-proofing seemed highly unlikely. We were *those* parents, the ones who practically hosed down visitors with antibacterial hand solution—and then refused to let them hold the baby. We installed tethers on the changing table, just in case our son—the one with no neck control—catapulted away from us, mid–diaper change. And when I took him for his first few walks, I actually slid the stroller wrist strap over my hand and tightened it around my forearm, in case a crazed baby snatcher tried to wrestle the stroller away from me on the mean streets of Cambridge, Massachusetts.

But, as time passed, and our son failed to spontaneously combust, we became more confident in our own skills and judgment. The complicated rituals that we relied upon to keep him safe no longer seemed necessary. In fact, they seemed preposterous.

So, when the topic of baby-proofing our home came up in my mothers' group, I hadn't given it much thought. My son was old enough that we measured his age in months rather than weeks but not old enough that he was able to move with any sort of intention. I figured we had plenty of time. Not true, the moderator of the group insisted. In hushed tones, she proceeded to spell out the hazards lurking in our homes and the tragedies that could befall our children if we didn't act: They could be crushed by unsecured furniture! Choke on loose change! Gouge themselves on sharp furniture corners!

Now, I have fears about my son. I worry that he'll be bullied in school or, worse, be a bully himself. I worry that he'll have half a million dollars in student debt. I worry he'll try coke with some kid named Travis in the parking lot of a Dave Matthews Band reunion concert.

But I'll be damned if I'm going to worry about him impaling himself on the coffee table.

Yet, among the other mothers in my group, panic was setting in. Brows furrowed, they volleyed questions to the moderator. Should they banish their household cleaners to the garage?

"But, as time passed, and our son failed to spontaneously combust, we became more confident in our own skills and judgment."

Cover the hardwoods with composite foam flooring? Replace the blinds with curtains?

The trend toward overzealous baby-proofing isn't isolated to the parents I know; it's everywhere. At the hardware store, there is an entire aisle dedicated to baby-proofing products. The array of plastic fixtures you can buy to secure your home is mind-blowing: magnetic cabinet locks, folding door latches, faucet covers, outlet covers, oven knob locks, cord wind-ups, bolts to secure your furniture to the walls, lockboxes for your cleaning products and medications, tubes for your wires, fences, gates, and—of course—furniture corner covers.

The message seems to be that childhood is a time of profound danger and that the only way to confront that danger is by adopting an all-consuming, hypervigilant style of parenting—and by spending lots of money. In fact, if you don't trust yourself to seek out and identify all the death-defying hazards in your home, you can spend hundreds of dollars hiring a company to come and baby-proof it for you.

I suppose if you are already replacing your plastic bottles with glass ones, forcing your doctor to agree to a revised vaccine schedule, and regularly checking the state sex-offender registry, then breaking out the power tools and tearing up your cabinets is just another day's parenting. But, for those of us who resist the idea that responsible child-rearing means driving yourself crazy, it is one more example of over-parenting gone mad.

Nevertheless, my husband and I thought about it. We could put safety bars on our windows and latches on our cabinets, we reasoned. We could scrub our floors each morning and nail the furniture to the walls. And, while we were at it, we could go back to being the kind of people who physically attach themselves to their child's stroller.

So, instead, we waited, as tummy time turned into tripod sitting, and batting toys turned into holding them. Crawling and climbing came next, followed by opening and shutting, dumping and spilling. Through all these phases, we have discovered that our son isn't Evel Knievel; he's just a kid who's curious about his world. And at no point have we felt that he is such a danger to himself that we have to build him a padded room.

Instead, we have discovered a real joy in watching our son interact with our things. His fascination with our stuff is far more rewarding than his passing interest in the plastic crap we've bought for him. Each morning, he shimmies over to our

Creature stereo subwoofer, which resides under my desk. He stares at it, palms it, occasionally tries to eat it. Then he turns the tiny silver knobs all the way up. Apparently, he thinks NPR could use a little more bass.

And I love that he prefers playing with our bookshelf to his own board book library. Sandra Boynton is perfectly entertaining, but my heart pitter-pats when I see him get up on tiptoes, haul *The Chicago Manual of Style* off the shelf, and sit quietly on the floor, flipping through its feather-thin pages.

Of course, we don't really think he is expressing a preference for high culture. He's exploring our things because they are colorful, or shaped to his liking; slap a pair of retractable googly-eyes on it, and the Creature is a dead ringer for Boohbah. Mostly, he gravitates to our stuff because it is ours and, in a way, by extension, his.

Nonetheless, we are perfectly aware that there are real dangers in our home, and we've addressed the ones that are genuinely threatening. We vacuum the floors every few days to collect the accumulation of detritus that he might otherwise ingest. We've learned to open our windows from the top, rather than the bottom. We would totally move the bleach to the back of the cabinet—if we actually owned bleach.

But, despite our best efforts, no level of baby-proofing will ever guarantee a child's safety. Sure enough, our son had his first choking scare just a few weeks ago, when he tried to swallow a part of one of his toys—and not just any toy: his handcrafted, age-appropriate, lead-paint-free, made-in-Vermont wooden bunny rabbit. He managed to chew off its little pink ear and was rolling it around in his mouth when my husband fished it out.

"... no level of baby-proofing will ever guarantee a child's safety."

Both inside the walls of our apartment and beyond it, there is a world that isn't always safe or healthy or perfect. And that's the world we are teaching our son to live in. So, there will be no composite foam flooring in our future. No spring-loaded outlet covers. No hours spent cursing each other as we try to affix all that plastic hardware. Our family is living life on the coffee table edge, so to speak. And we couldn't be happier about it.

nude awakening:
Am I Scarring My Kids by Walking Around Naked?

Emily Mendell

My ten-year-old son storms into my bedroom, plants his feet, fixes his eyes on me, and bellows, "I can't take it anymore. He won't stop banging his drums when I'm trying to play Guitar Hero! Can you *pleeeeeeeease* help me? *Now*?"

"Sure—just give me two secs."

He huffs back toward the playroom, glancing over his shoulder at me to make sure I am on my way to save him from his younger brother. A typical exchange between mother and son, with one exception: I am completely naked.

He caught me coming out of the shower at the precise moment when the wet towel went up on the hook and I was figuring out what to wear that day. The bedroom door was open, and I was routing through my underwear drawer, still bare, when confronted with his urgent problem. Yet, neither one of us skipped a beat. I may as well have been standing there in a full-length parka, boots, and a hat. It was a nonevent for both of us.

Later, I ask my husband, "Do you think it's creepy that I still let the boys see me without clothes on?"

"It's not creepy. It's not like you prance around or anything."

"So, as long as there is no prancing, it's okay?"

"I think so."

"What about when they're teenagers?"

"You might want to rethink things then."

But I don't want to rethink things. There are certain inalienable rights associated with the family. For me, nudity is one of them.

My feelings are not rooted politically. I am not taking any sort of stand on freedom of expression. And I'm certainly not making bold statements about "not being ashamed of my body." At thirty-nine years old, I clearly sport some body parts that are worthy of a little shame. But I am closer to these humans than to anybody else in the entire world. If, so to speak, they are the fruit of my loins, why should I have to rush to cover said loins?

A strong case can be made that when your children are toddlers, nudity is not negotiable. When flying solo with my kids, my trips to the bathroom and shower were rarely unaccompanied. Doors were never locked. Unfettered access was a safety issue. But somewhere around age four or five, that argument no longer holds water. It's at this point that parents choose how they want things to be.

I chose not to cover up—and am sticking with that decision—because paranoia regarding nudity in my own home feels repressive. Yet, it remains an incredible quandary for me and the

countless other parents who have young children of the opposite sex. My husband can walk around the house buck naked
for the rest of his life without question or judgment because his
parts match our children's. My sister, the mother of two daughters, can do the same. Yet, as a mother of brothers, my nakedness
might be questioned. It feels unfair.

"I remember seeing both my parents naked when I was a child—never out of context and never in an inappropriate way. I don't feel the least bit scarred by this."

Fathers of daughters have it far worse. The stigma of who is
and who isn't a sexual predator falls more heavily on men. I find
myself thinking often of *The Good Mother*, the Sue Miller–novel-
turned-movie with Diane Keaton and Liam Neeson, in which a

mother's custody is threatened when her young daughter sees her boyfriend naked and asks to touch his penis. The boyfriend, with actually the best intentions, agrees, and all hell breaks loose. Clearly, in this scenario, a line was crossed. But who draws the line?

Nudity in the family falls under the same guidelines as how long to breast-feed, how much TV gets watched, or whether sugar cereal is available for breakfast. It varies by family and, I imagine, lines up very closely with what the parents experienced as children. I remember seeing both my parents naked when I was a child—never out of context and never in an inappropriate way. I don't feel the least bit scarred by this. Conversely, married friends of ours who were both raised in conservative households never saw their parents naked. Consequently, they are never unclothed in front of their own children. I suspect they stay covered up in front of the family pets, too.

Expert opinions on this particular topic may be out there, but finding them online is another story. I went to Google "nudity, children" and then thought twice before hitting "I'm Feeling Lucky." I don't need Chris Hansen showing up in my kitchen. But my concern speaks directly to how stigmatized we have become.

Truth be told, I am not immune to the moral barometer. To wit, showers with Mommy were at one point a special treat for my little guys. There was nothing inappropriate about this activity whatsoever, in my opinion. I washed their hair, made bubbles, and helped rinse. They didn't wash me. But, one day, I noticed that they were tall enough that eye level for them was crotch level on me. And the shower stall does not leave a great deal of room for personal space. That was the day the Mommy showers stopped.

While I hold my ground on my right to be naked around my kids, I do think there are certain parameters by which to abide:

1) I will not force my nudity on my children. Except for the rare occasion when I need to retrieve some critical article of clothing from the downstairs laundry room and decide to make a dash for it alfresco, my nakedness will remain in the bedroom and bathroom, where I have a right not to be paranoid about it. If they stumble upon me in a state of undress, so be it. If they don't want to get an eyeful, they will learn to knock.

2) I will never be naked in front of their friends. I do not aspire to be Stifler's mom. When guests are in the house, I will stay covered.

3) If I am going to put myself out there like that, I am going to have to be willing to answer their questions when asked. So far, there haven't been that many queries, but I probably should practice saying the word "vagina" a lot more.

4) No touching, tickling, hugging, kissing, back scratching, or wrestling naked. While these are activities that we do engage in regularly when everyone is dressed, doing any of these things while clothes are off feels highly inappropriate. So, it probably is.

5) Lastly, and most importantly, I will trust my gut. We ask our own children to do the same when it comes to protecting themselves. When something doesn't feel right, it almost certainly isn't. My choice to let my kids see me naked is always reversible. I can just simply start covering up. (For the record, I don't think the same can be said if your children have never seen you nude and you suddenly decide to expand their horizons.)

I would never judge another parent who is uncomfortable with nudity. I would ask her to do the same with me. With all the horrible things we hear about happening to children, it is no wonder we have become a society of overly paranoid parents. It is one thing not to trust others with your children. It is another thing not to trust yourself. The fact that my son doesn't bat an eye at my unclad body suggests that I am raising an uninhibited child, who has the highest level of comfort with his mother. In my opinion, there isn't anything creepy about that.

anger management:
I Lose My Temper, and I Think That's Okay

Sarah Irwin

My hands are shaking. It's 3 AM, and I have been bouncing on the balls of my feet since 1:30. The sweaty, twenty-pound bulk of my nine-month-old son slumps against my shoulder. Suddenly, he pushes away from my chest, his body clenched, a prolonged scream escaping. My bouncing turns jerky, and my arms squeeze too tight, forcing another scream out of him, this time one of protest. My mantra for the past half hour will not leave my head: *I hate this. I can't do this anymore. I hate this.*

I have to put him down. When I lean him over the side of his crib, his body tenses and a wail rises in his throat.

"I'm sorry, Will," I say. I clumsily lay him down, and he screams. As I crumble into bed, every nerve in my body is on edge. The wails next door pulsate, and I imagine I'm never going to sleep again.

Before I had my son, my images of motherhood always included a rocking chair—a mother with an infant cradled in her arms. Of course, babies cried and got upset, but mothers soothed. I knew parenting would drive me to frustration, but I would never be like those bad mothers at the mall who yelled at and spanked their screaming children. So, it was a shock to me the first time I felt the passion rising, the desire to squeeze him just a little too hard, wanting to cause him some of the agony he was causing me.

When Will was just twelve hours old, my husband, Dave, and I couldn't stop staring at him. When a nurse remarked that he looked like Harold from the children's book *Harold and the Purple Crayon*, I flushed with new motherly pride. When he wasn't sleeping, his eyes opened wide with what seemed a happy, almost cartoonish curiosity, his tiny nose sloped up in perfection, pale wisps of fuzz on his head. His head nuzzled against Dave's chest, his tiny fist clenched, we watched him in silence.

"I don't understand how anyone could ever hurt a child," Dave said, his voice suddenly heated. I murmured in agreement, my body tense at the thought. During those first few days at the hospital, I had vivid images of my wrinkled and cooing newborn hurt in some way—I would close my eyes and see his arm broken, his face turning purple, or his body falling out of a high-rise window. Perhaps it was the powerful postpartum hormones surging through my body, the primordial nature of motherhood.

I would shake my head to clear away the horrible images, chastising myself for such awful thoughts.

He was so vulnerable. A living being, body and soul, who, without the assistance of another, could not eat or even move. Without me, awful things just might happen to him.

The first weeks on the job quickly changed my idyllic image of myself. When a night with five straight hours of sleep seemed an impossible miracle, when his screaming caused my blood pressure to rise and my nervous system to go haywire, the discovery scared me: I could be the one to harm him.

Perhaps this shouldn't have come as such a surprise. My mother, whose fiery extremes I inherited, once broke my brother's eardrum. He had sassed at something she said, and she smacked him across the head. It was the 1970s, and the subsequent hospital visit resulted in no questioning of my parents. My brother described his earache to the doctor, a diagnosis was made, and antibiotic drops were prescribed. My mom only mentioned it to me once or twice—her voice quiet, face flushed.

Anger is not new to me, and I knew Will would eventually evoke it. I was just surprised it came so soon, before he was even capable of sitting up. Amidst all the baby showers, tiny sweaters and socks, plush blankets and stuffed toys, our image of babies is all tenderness. We hear so much about the joys of "little ones" that images contrary to that notion seem somehow wrong. When I was pregnant, mothers with grown children told me of the instant mother-child bond, of tightly curled fingers and toes, of how peaceful his warm sleeping body would feel against my chest. No one told me my anger would make me, at times, want to hurt him.

"To feel anger toward a child, particularly a baby, is something most new parents hide."

To feel anger toward a child, particularly a baby, is something most new parents hide. Especially in an age of over-parenting perfection, we pride ourselves on being so well-read and educated that bumps in the road are our own fault, stemming only from our own ignorance. We know much more than parents of the past. We know the harm that expressing our anger can cause. We have seen children ravaged by anger turned violent, their stories a dull ache in our chests. But this still can't make our own anger, when summoned, suddenly disappear.

Most of my friends refused to admit they had these feelings, preferring to segue into a conversation about "those cute little toes," but my friend Kate, thirty-two, a high school English teacher and mother of a three-year-old, told me, "There is no way of reasoning with a screaming baby or a tantrum-throwing toddler. I have literally had to put my daughter into the backseat of the car, close the door, and walk in circles around the car so that I don't do something I will regret."

She agreed that being angry at your children somehow seemed more permissible in years past. "It used to be okay to spank, it used to be okay to scream, so people felt less ashamed of their actions. The mores are much stricter today—and probably rightfully so—but we also don't know what we are supposed to do with our anger."

Even though we have been taught that anger toward a child, more often than not, is inappropriate, changing norms can't alter base human emotions. And just why is anger so maligned? Are we doing our children any favors by hiding our own anger, or perhaps letting it out in passive ways that are ultimately just as harmful as, if not more so, than a spanking?

Searching my local library's database, I found shelves of parenting advice, with titles like *The Wonder Years, Smart Love,* and *The Confident Child.* When it came to anger, however, there was not much to be found. Beyond the outdated *Battles, Hassles, Tantrums, and Tears: Strategies for Coping with Conflict and Making Peace at Home* (a Good Housekeeping Parent Guide; the clip-art image on the cover shows an alarm clock ringing while a mother with pearl earrings pulls at her child's arm, attempting to get him out of bed), the only book I found dealing directly with parental anger was *Love and Anger: The Parental Dilemma,* by Nancy Samalin.

Samalin notes that children bring "warmth, humor, boundless energy, and creativity" to a household, but "by their nature . . . bring to the family environment disorder, aggravation, ambiguity, and turmoil" as well. She goes on to note that "many people find it hard to accept that such an intensity of negative feelings could be radiating from them to their (normally) beloved, innocent children. If our capacity to feel terrible anger for the children we love distresses us, it is our capacity to speak and act from those angry feelings that so often fills us with horror and self-loathing."

But is it fair for us always to deny our own extremes, or to loathe ourselves for being human in the midst of such a challenging job? A friend with three children under the age of seven puts it this way: being drawn into a confrontation with your child is like being drawn into a confrontation with your own mother—you know it's probably the better choice to step away, but there's a child in you that wants to be angry.

Parents are not emotionless robots. If we were, we would not know the abounding love only a parent can have for a child. Unfortunately, along with that come raw edges, which can only serve as constant reminders of our profound inability to reach parental perfection. And perhaps this isn't such an awful thing. My brother, today a successful family physician, has received many awards and accolades over the years, and with every one, his imperfect mother beamed with pride.

game over: I Hate Playing with My Kids

Shelley Abreu

"You be Ariel, and I'll be Prince Eric," instructs my three-year-old daughter, Julia. Then she dives down into the pretend ocean that is our kitchen floor and beckons me to save her. I scoop her in my arms, and we swim safely to "Ariel's Grotto." I attempt to return to chopping vegetables, but she begins the game again. I try to get out of it. "Ariel has to cook up some crabs for Prince Eric's supper," I say. But she's onto me. "Ariel doesn't cook the supper," she retorts.

It's not the first time today I've dodged Julia's games. After a short stint playing a mind-numbing game of Candy Land: Dora the Explorer, I fake a bathroom emergency. When I come out, I casually begin folding laundry. When Julia calls me back to the game, I tell her I'll come back soon. I'm lying.

Sometimes I'm not even that suave about averting playtime with Julia. After a few laps around the house playing tag, I simply run away mid-lap. For a moment, it delights her when she realizes I'm missing. She thinks I've turned it into a game of hide-and-seek, but after a few minutes she begs me to return. Then I use my arsenal of verbal excuses, including: I need to get the house picked up and make a phone call. When she whines, I urge her to play with her younger sister, Elise, who is old enough to toddle her way through a round of any running game. And that's what siblings are for, right?

I'm not a complete failure at playing. I'm content to do puzzles, and I'll take time out from any adult activity to read a book. I'm a musician, which means anything musical is pretty much okay with me. I'll also last a good while at I Spy during walks through our neighborhood. But, generally speaking, I hate playing with my kids. Games of "Horsey," in which I'm asked to giddyap through our yard, or "Payer," where we use a toy cash register to enact pretend transactions, are enough to make me lose my mind. Of all the negatives that parenting has brought—sleep deprivation, a constantly messy house, nary a moment to myself—it's the playing that I hate the most.

And yet, read any mainstream parenting magazine today, and you're made to believe that playing with your children is essential to their well-being. I recently read "Fidgety Kids: 10 Fun Games You Can Play in an Instant." The article suggests I pass the time waiting at the pediatrician's office by using the exam-table paper to draw a village. It's not that I can't appreciate the inventiveness of this crafty game, but, truthfully, I'd rather read a magazine and let my kids entertain themselves with the germy toys (which, by the way, they love).

Another recent article suggests that at holiday get-togethers, adults take all the children outside and enjoy a jaunty game of monkey-in-the-middle. I don't know about you, but when we have get-togethers around our house, we let the kids play with each other while the adults enjoy festive drinks. In his book *Raise a Smarter Child by Kindergarten*, Dr. David Perlmutter hails the importance of playing with our children to promote intelligence and, in support, offers pages of tedious activities.

" . . . truthfully, I'd rather read a magazine and let my kids entertain themselves . . . . "

Luckily, the jury's still out. The *Boston Globe* recently reported that playing with your children is actually a modern phenomenon and not necessarily all that beneficial. According to anthropological studies, three-fourths of the world's parents don't participate in the kind of parent-child play so popular in our current American culture. In fact, an article titled "Leave Those Kids Alone" suggests that most cultures think we're kind of nutty.

Still, deep down, I consider playing with my kids something I should do. Not because I think it will raise their IQs or because it will make me a better mother, but because they want me to. After all, what's so hard about sitting down for a tea party with twelve furry stuffed animals and two cute little girls? Maybe it's the fact that, as a mother who works from home, I have so much to do every day that squandering twenty minutes on fake tea and pretend friends—while I think about unanswered e-mails and piles of laundry—makes me fidgety.

And when I think back to my own childhood, I don't recall my parents ever playing with me or my brother. He and I played together, building elaborate forts, rescuing stray animals, hunting for frogs, and thinking up creative ways to execute my Barbies. Would we have done any of this if my mother had been right there orchestrating elaborate games instead? I don't think so. So, I'm going to follow her lead. I'll stick to the grown-up things—making a living, picking up toys, doing dishes, vacuuming floors—and I'll let the kids have fun for all of us. Although I may not care to swim around the house dressed up as Ariel the mermaid, I'm happy to do all the things that allow my daughters the time and space so that they can.

straight to the bottle: I Decided Not to Breast-Feed

Tricia Grissom

After my second child was born, I decided I wanted my boobs back. It was a long journey, learning I deserved my boobs. Everyone told me they belonged to my babies. When my daughter was born three years ago, I tried breast-feeding her but stopped when she didn't gain weight. I felt less guilty about my first attempt than my second effort with my son. After all, he wasn't losing weight yet—no more than a normal newborn, anyway. He started at a healthy 9 lbs. 7 oz., so he wasn't exactly wasting away.

And breast-feeding was apparently the pinnacle of motherhood. All the mothering tomes I read disagreed on many things—co-sleeping, solid foods, how to remove beans from the nose—but on one subject they were unanimous: if you didn't breast-feed, you were obviously a lazy, bonbon-eating mommy who couldn't be bothered to properly nourish your baby. How could anyone possibly want anything but the best for her baby? And indisputably, the best thing was breast-feeding.

But I hated it. It got to where I didn't want to hold my son anymore because it was a job, not an adventure in getting to know him. And the sleep, my god the sleep! I craved it like an addict. I sneaked naps sitting on the bathroom toilet. I caressed my bed longingly as I walked by, buried my nose in the covers, and imagined a time machine that would let me sleep for three days solid without causing my son to starve. I ambled around the house while my three-year-old tried to identify this zombie who used to read books to and tickle her—and figure out why the zombie always had a hungry, crying appendage attached to her chest.

I was caught up in the whole vicious circle: baby always wanting to nurse, me not having enough milk, baby always wanting to nurse. I felt like a twenty-four-hour grocery store at the apocalypse—under-stocked and trying to keep the customers from rioting.

My lactation consultant—a warm, sympathetic woman— calmly talked me down as I sobbed into the phone in my doctor's private office while my three-year-old destroyed every anatomical model in sight. I gently chastised my daughter to stop, held my newborn, clutched the phone to my ear, and tried to figure out what was wrong with me that I couldn't manage to do this thing women had done for thousands of years. The lactation consultant praised me for being so patient with my daughter. She didn't know what I was actually thinking: *I can get rid of my first child. After all, I have a spare now, right?*

All those burgeoning post-pregnancy hormones rose up to make me a blubbering mess. I sat in the office crying, holding, distracting, and dissolving. The consultant suggested buying a breast pump and pumping every four hours to increase milk production. So, I bought the expensive pump at the medical supply store, even though we could barely afford it. Every night, I tried to feed my son as he woke every two to three hours, and then got up again to pump on the four-hour schedule.

My husband couldn't do any of it for me. The experts warned against giving supplementary bottles, claiming the baby would become accustomed to the fake nipple. I doubted this. But I didn't know if I could stand losing to the synthetic version of me, so I got up every two hours most nights.

In the evolutionary sense, I felt like a total failure. My genetic profile was too weak to survive. My DNA did not deserve to go on. My son was losing IQ points every minute because I couldn't squirt out enough nourishment to grow his brain cells efficiently. He could have been secretary of state, but because of me he would work in a video store.

And the pumping wasn't working. I called the lactation consultant again, and she suggested a medication that might improve milk production. I filled the prescription with total despair. I took one chalky pill, and then I stopped. I couldn't do it anymore. I put away the breast pump, and I threw away the pills. I was done. It had been decided. I was a bad mother, and I was going to embrace it. What was next? Soda in the baby bottle or putting him to sleep facedown? Decisions, decisions.

I felt guilty every day. But, slowly, I also started to feel like a person again. I was possessive of my breasts now. It was time

"I couldn't do it anymore. I put away the breast pump, and I threw away the pills. I was done."

for us to get reacquainted. I got out my non-nursing bra and penned up my breasts for an entire day. No flaps were unflapped, no snaps unsnapped. On his new formula regimen, my son fell into a sound sleep that lasted five blissful hours.

I went out to lunch and lingered over dessert instead of circling home like a mother pigeon with hungry mouths to feed. There was room on my lap for my first child. She had not adjusted well to having a baby brother permanently attached to my chest. Now I could make it up to her and convince her that the baby wasn't a space alien sucking the life out of her mother. She stopped peeing on the floor of her room to get my attention. All was well in the world.

And one day, when my mother walked in holding my son, I was struck by an unfamiliar urge. I wanted to hold him. I wanted to hold him and just be his mother. Not the mother who had to feed him, but the mother who just wanted to look at how beautiful he was. I actually wanted him in my arms instead of wanting to hide from him.

At first, I felt guilty about my breast-feeding breakdown. Without the miracle of modern formula, my kids would have died. I didn't have what it took to ensure the survival of my species. But, years later, I realized the truth. When my level of suffering became so great that I considered faking a spontaneous coma to get some rest, it was much better for my son to have a plugged in, adoring mother than a milk shake dispenser. I didn't feel guilty anymore.

I hear the pro-breast-feeding camp mission to new mothers, and I smile serenely. Nutritionally deprived my children may be, but I can look them in their IQ-challenged little faces and not want to sell them to the gypsies. And I can live with that.

raising the bar: I Washed My Child's Mouth Out with Soap

Kris Malone Grossman

It all began in the driveway, when my four-year-old, Leo, was learning to ride his bike. He'd grow frustrated and scream, "Stupid, stupid, stupid!" when he couldn't manipulate the pedals quickly enough, especially when his older brother tore past and dusted him. I puffed up with pride: I'd taught Leo to express his anger.

Then he turned the "stupid" on me.

Generally, I'm the kind of parent who shrugs off outbursts—an effective strategy with my first, who's all head. No such personality my middle, all-heart child, Leo. The more I ignore him, the louder he shrieks and the meaner he gets. Now, I can understand the outrage of being blown off after giving a dramatic, motion-picture-worthy tantrum. What I don't get, however, is where Leo picked up the word "stupid" in the first place, or how he ever stumbled onto the fantasy he describes of chopping me up with a knife and throwing my bones "into a tree."

Granted, I did read *In Cold Blood* when I was pregnant with Leo. And I've likely slung around the word "stupid" in front of him once or twice—but never in regard to a person (not within earshot, anyway) and never attached to a dismemberment fantasy. In any case, Leo has thrown a wrench into my understanding of myself as a totally laissez-faire, it'll-pass mother, the kind who adheres to the Summerhill-esque philosophy that, when left to their own devices, kids inevitably correct themselves.

"But when he started screaming, 'Stupid Mommy!' nonstop, something in me snapped."

None of my usual tricks were working, so I decided to go corporal with the oldest, least PC discipline technique I could think of: washing his mouth out with soap.

Believe me, it wasn't easy. The very thought of it made me consider turning myself in to Child Protective Services. But, one day, I was pushed over the edge.

I'd just informed Leo he could not bite his brothers, and he turned his fangs on me. Before he could sink them in, I packed him up the stairs to serve a time-out in his bedroom (door open, toys allowed). But when he started screaming, "Stupid Mommy!" nonstop, something in me snapped. Maybe it was that, while screaming, he tried to kick me, or that, during all of this, I was balancing his howling baby brother on my hip. Or maybe it was that he announced yet again that he was going to kill me and toss my body parts in the woods. Maybe it was insult fatigue. Maybe I was especially mad because the day had been so lovely until that point. I'd just lovingly assembled another snack of farm-fresh berries, washed the favorite T. rex T-shirt for the gazillionth time, and passed the morning spending quality time with Leo rock-throwing and aster-hunting in nearby woods.

But, all those factors, combined with the rigors (noise pollution, constant body mauling) of raising three boys under the age of six made me snap.

Leo sniffed danger when I returned after leaving him in his room, an ominous reversal of time-out protocol. At first, he ventured an innocent, "What are you doing in here?" When I didn't answer and continued to advance, he went ahead and yelled, "Stupid Mommy!" Predictably, when I flashed the soap, he retreated and cowered with eyes so wide and sweet they could have been culled from a "Child abuse hurts everyone" poster you'd see tacked in a doctor's office.

Any hesitation on my part was wiped out by another scream of "Stupid Mommy!" I put the soap on his tongue and rubbed it around. After a few rounds, he stopped and stared at the soap.

"Stupid Mommy?"

Back went the soap.

While washing my kid's mouth out with soap doesn't fit my definition of cruel and unusual punishment, it still feels eerily like wielding the rod and sending a kid to bed without supper. I have friends who fall on both ends of the discipline spectrum, from those who defend the occasional slap on the hand or smack on the behind (about which I've been self-righteously outraged) to ponytailed softies who espouse the practice of hugging their "spirited" kids into "submission," then rewarding them with rice cream.

Like my parents, who spanked me just twice (for coaxing all the neighborhood kids into playing doctor), then gave it up, I fall closer to the lax, rice cream extreme. As for my husband, his father used to make him hold out his hands after particularly egregious transgressions, then rap his knuckles. When my husband confessed the anticipation was more humiliating than the smack itself, I made him promise we would never, ever spank our kids.

So, why does soap in the mouth seem okay to me? Maybe because the practice, popular during the 1940s and 1950s, seems antique in a good way. When it comes to parenting these days, old school is new school: glass bottles, cloth diapers, and no more late-twentieth-century nice-nice, when guilt-addicted parents dished up enough permissiveness and positive reinforcement to render entire generations inept at processing even the gentlest criticism. By not correcting our kids, we leave them vastly underprepared to cope with the real world.

Not everyone is so gung ho about my new parenting tool. I've asked everyone what they think: my parents, my friends, my husband, my mentors, my shrink, even strangers in the street. I've consulted books. And I've considered their myriad, sage counter-suggestions: Ignore the bad behavior, give strokes for the good. Use time-outs. Count. Remember, it's just a phase.

"Which brings us to the best argument in favor of the soap: it worked."

Listen, love, hug. Use motivating sticker charts. Take Leo for special outings. Give him words. Let him be. Imagine fitting him with an electric-fence collar, like a dog's, that will gently jolt him whenever he crosses the line. And let's not leave out my favorite, posited by my husband: when Leo flips, get into the car, and just "drive off somewhere." (And leave our five-year-old to babysit Leo and the baby?)

To be sure, I could probably expend a lot more energy working with Leo to get him to bag the bad language. But I've got two other kids to corral. And while I can unleash all host of wily psychological tricks or leave Leo to writhe solo in his favored kitchen corner, while I can continue to best my temper and set limits and be the Mommy Who Rarely Yells and exhaust all the enlightened, attachment parenting avenues that allow him to express his feelings in a safe, loving environment, at a certain point, it's time to lay down the law.

Which brings us to the best argument in favor of the soap: it worked. It's been almost a week now—one whole, glorious, "Stupid Mommy"-free week. Leo's still acting out, though less, and more importantly, he's curbed his tongue. The baby is bite-free. My husband recovered his voice, which he'd lost from yelling so much. So, please, spare me the talk of allowing Leo to share his feelings and, "Oh, the poor darling, he's a middle child and you crushed him by having another baby and you should spend more time with him and, by the way, you need to see a shrink."

Hooey on all that. Tough being in the middle? Suck it up. Hate me? That's okay, I still love you, enough to sling custom dinner plates and give you super snuggles and conduct house-wide hunts at bedtime for Little Bear, every day, any day, for as long as we both shall live. But it's also my job to make sure Leo learns that it's not okay to call me, or anyone else, names. To that end, I have to do whatever it takes.

my baby was a cover girl: I Stage-Mothered My Infant

April Peveteaux

Before I gave birth, I viewed babies with a critical eye, the same one that judged *Beauty and the Geek* contestants. Sure, I thought all babies were cute in that *E.T.* kind of way, but I wouldn't have called a three-day-old gorgeous. I believed kids needed to be at least two years old so you could see how their hair was going to work with their face. Seriously, I said that. But that was before I gave birth to my own old-man-looking, chicken-legged little squirmer. In the delivery room, I was fitted with my own pair of rose-colored glasses, and I knew she was the most beautiful baby in the universe. But even I was surprised when a modeling agent agreed.

When I became pregnant, my fledgling acting career (that was me playing the bank secretary in *Law & Order*'s season 9, episode 23) came to a halt. A friend of mine suggested I do some pregnant modeling, so I signed with an agency that specialized in pregnant models and babies. And I didn't think anything of it that, when I gave birth, my baby girl, Esmé, went into their headshot files.

"Every month, we flipped through magazines at the stand to see her latest photos. . . . Cautionary tales, like Drew Barrymore and JonBenét Ramsey, flew out of my head."

Esmé booked her first job at three months. And, unlike me, this girl had nerves of steel. She greeted the cast of dozens—stylist, makeup artist, photo assistants—with that winning smile. As we arrived at that first job, a magazine representative greeted us and ushered us over to the stylist, who sized up Esmé, pulled out a fancy little blue outfit, and gave us strict instructions to keep her bibbed and as still as possible to protect the garment from drool and wrinkles. Next, the hair-and-makeup guy took one look at Esmé and declared her ready. Apparently, concealer isn't necessary when your skin has only been exposed to the elements for ninety days. I wondered how much he made for chirping, "Babies are perfect the way they are!"

As we sat and waited for the photographer to finish setting the stage, I noticed a few other babies arriving. I asked one mom what she was there for, as if, perhaps, she had gotten lost along the West Side Highway and thought this was a good place to stop and nurse. She told me she was there for the same shoot—and, by the way, was my daughter sleeping through the night? Before I had a chance to lie, she called over a three-year-old girl who had been pirouetting around the room, black hair swishing luxuriously around her shoulders. "She's also a model," her mother said. "She's done Gap, Ralph Lauren, and Enfamil." The little girl smiled and tilted her head in a perfect Breck Girl pose. I knew if her baby sister was half as talented, Esmé was in trouble.

Baby modeling feeds on this kind of competition. Smart casting directors will hire anywhere from three to five babies to do one job. That's because baby models tend to spit up on wardrobe, get painful gas, or take impromptu naps. You still get paid for your time, anywhere from $50 to $200 an hour, but, if you wind up in print, you also get a usage fee, which can hit four figures. I didn't much care about the money, but the condescending mother with the perfect little girls had me ready to rumble.

When the set was ready, one of the photo assistants came into the waiting room. "Are any of the babies asleep?" she asked. I proudly announced, "No!" Esmé hardly ever napped for more than fifteen minutes at a time. Another mother said her baby was, indeed, sleeping. *Loser!* I thought. We had this in the bag! But then the assistant said to the other mother, "Great. Mom, can you bring her to the set?" A crib had been assembled to receive only sleeping baby models.

Desperate, I borrowed another mom's stroller to roll Esmé around the hallway. For two hours, I wheeled her up and down. Eventually, Esmé succumbed. I grabbed her and ran into the studio. The crew got some lovely shots in the ten minutes before she woke up. A few months later, I picked up *Parents* magazine and there was Esmé, illustrating an article about SIDS sure to terrify thousands of new parents. We were ecstatic.

Soon after came the second job, then the third. By the fifth gig, my husband and I were in shock. Every month, we flipped through magazines at the stand to see her latest photos. We would look back and forth between the ad and the real deal, smiling our heads off. My mother-in-law's reaction encapsulated what we all were thinking: "We knew she was beautiful, but this *proves* it!" Even my mother, who is from Oklahoma, where it's illegal to draw attention to yourself, loved going to the newsstand and seeing her granddaughter smiling out at her. Cautionary tales, like Drew Barrymore and JonBenét Ramsey, flew out of my head.

Clearly, Esmé had a gift. As long as there was a colorful toy, Esmé was good. She had no idea why people shone a light in her eyes and shook rattles while talking in a maniacally high-pitched voice, but she didn't seem to mind. She could keep smiling after three wardrobe changes under the hot lights of a cold studio. I had never been that patient. I wondered: *Would she grow up to gain all the fame I never had? What would have come of me if I had gotten such an early start? Had such a supportive mother?* I thought of all the times my father would say I should enter the pageant circuit and my mother would respond, "Absolutely not." Watching Esmé enjoy her work, I wondered if I should have been allowed to enter the world of silicone and Vaseline.

Then, we hit the big time: Pampers. Esmé had been fighting a fever for a few days, but that morning she seemed back to her happy-go-lucky self—until we got to the audition. In the waiting room, she began to look not so good, and I don't mean her hair. She was shaking, and her lips and cheeks were purplish blue. (I would later find out this was a fever spike.) I was trying to get a read on whether the fever was back or if this was an allergic reaction, when the coordinator approached me to ask, "Are you okay?"

I looked down at Esmé. If I answered, "Yes," and brought my shivering daughter into the room, I would be casting myself in a future memoir, *Mommie Dearest Redux.* If I left, we would miss a big opportunity and risk being labeled "flaky." I went with flaky. I wrapped up my daughter and said, "No."

On our way home from the doctor's office, where Esmé was treated for an ear infection, I wondered if I'd crossed the line into psychotic stage mother. Sure, in the past I'd canceled my baby's playgroup so she could be rested and ready for an afternoon shoot, but this time I'd actually taken her to a casting call even though she was sick. I wondered if that was a sign that it was time to quit. She'd made more than $2,000 (enough that she had to pay taxes before her first birthday), and she'd had a four-month run in one national magazine. My husband and I had long discussions about what would be best for her. But, in the end, it didn't matter how we felt about it. After we skipped that Pampers audition, we never heard from Esmé's agent again.

birthday parties gone wild: Limo? Check. Tiger Cub? Check. My Son Having Fun? Uh . . .

Asra Q. Nomani

As I turned the page of my local newspaper not long ago, I read a story about a new self-help group in which I could have been a charter member: Birthdays Without Pressure. The group is made up of recovering over-the-top-party throwers and those disgusted by party excess. The trend toward ever-grander parties has led, the group says, to such a sense of entitlement, young guests are apt to yell, "This is a rip-off!" at a birthday party without gift bags.

Here's my shameful confession: for my son's first birthday, I rented a newborn tiger cub from a local county zoo (cost: $200 for two hours; my enabling friend Lynn picked up the bill). My lame justification: my son's name, Shibli, means "my lion cub," and, yes, I first asked for lion cubs. For his second birthday,

I had custom-designed invitations ($42.20), rented a barn at a place called Rich Farm outside of town, and booked a hayride and karaoke machine (final price tag: about $300). For his third birthday, I rented a white stretch limo ($300) and had the driver take us to a home recording studio ($275), where my son cut his first CD, belting out the "Dump Truck Song," with his own lyrics. It went something like this: "Dump truck! Dump truck! DUMP TRUCK! DUMP TRUCK!"

Each year, I asked my mother for a simple favor, a piece of cake for any doting immigrant grandma from India: "Can you cook *biryani* for, oh, say, fifty people? Oh, and can you be sure to have it all done beforehand so you can, you know, have fun at your grandson's birthday party?" Each year, she obliged, saving me hundreds on catering that could then be spent on the next extravagance.

Before Shibli turned four, I watched with envy as parents of a preschool pal hosted their son Cole's third birthday party with cupcakes and grilled cheese sandwiches for the children, who played happily with the birthday boy's regular, everyday toys. My son was thrilled pushing a fire engine and taking home a party bag with knicknacks. The whole thing couldn't have cost more than $50. And Cole's parents were chill throughout, chatting with the grown-ups. Could throwing a birthday party really be that easy? I resolved to restrain myself.

And restrain myself I did—until the eve of Shibli's fourth birthday party, when I panicked and pulled an all-nighter, downloading pirate-theme ideas all night long to create a complicated scheme consisting of gangplanks, treasure chests, and treasure hunts. At the craft store, it wasn't enough for me to get

"... I panicked and pulled an all-nighter, downloading pirate-theme ideas all night long to create a complicated scheme consisting of gang-planks, treasure chests, and treasure hunts."

the ninety-nine-cent treasure chests. I had to get the $2.99 ones. And I couldn't just get the store-decorated cake; I had to put up masts myself on a pirate-ship cake. "Where are the skewers?" I asked a clerk, almost breathless from my sprint through the store's aisles, mere hours before party time.

Of course, at cake time, Shibli was more interested in a new Polly Pocket gizmo than eating a slice. And the masts were so lopsided, the cake looked more like a shipwreck.

According to the quiz on the Birthdays Without Pressure Web site, I scored eighteen out of twenty points. Their verdict: "Have 911 on speed dial at your next party."

At least I'm not alone. Birthday parties gone wild are part of the cultural zeitgeist of Gen X parents like me. On its Web site, Birthdays Without Pressure has listed some three hundred pieces on the trend, appearing everywhere from the *Poughkeepsie Journal* to BBC World Service, with headlines like "My Super Sweet Six: Don't You Wish Your Birthday Party Was Hot Like Mine?" The *Irish Independent* called birthdays gone wild "Posh Party Syndrome" and described Victoria "Posh Spice" Beckham's daughter, Brooklyn's, fifth birthday party, which featured champagne (for the parents) and a DJ. The *Norwich Bulletin* in Connecticut chronicled "Supersize Birthday Parties." A columnist in the *Virginian-Pilot* exclaimed, "A stretch limo for a seven-year-old? Please!"

I couldn't agree more. Stretch limos after the age of five are so tacky.

The children's birthday party business has become a multi-million-dollar industry. Paper plates come with every conceivable theme because colored paper plates just aren't good enough anymore. The competition factor is huge. The April 2007 issue of *FamilyFun* magazine featured a photo of a grinning redhead with a balloon, across which was emblazoned, *Birthday Blowout!* The cover story: "Secrets of Great Parties!"

But for whom are we having these birthdays? It goes without saying that it's about us, not our children. I know from where my impulse comes: guilt about being a working mom, projected ambition, a desire to be the "fun mom." With slumber parties and other "cool" American social habits foreign to my own mother, I'm going overboard creating my own idea of what a fun mom looks like.

As we drove to gymnastics practice the other day, I asked my son, "Do you remember the baby tiger from your first birthday?"

His answer: "What tiger?"

How about the party on the farm?

"Farm?" he answered.

The limo. How about the limo? Do you remember what color it was?

"Green?"

Okay, touché. What does he remember from his last birthday? "The pirate cake." Yes, the shipwreck. And what would he like to do for his fifth birthday party?

"Play," he answered quickly. "And we get to do whatever we want to do."

Grilled cheese sandwiches and Legos it is.

love you, hate your kid: How Could I Feel So Little Affection for My Friend's Three-Year-Old?

Evie wanted to see the baby. I was reluctant to let her. My ten-day-old daughter had just recovered from a mucus-heavy cold that made her breathing and my sleeping irregular and difficult. My friend's daughter, Evie, had been around the wet, germy breath of preschoolers all day, and there was a month left until the end of flu season. But it was hard for me to say no, even to a three-year-old I didn't actually like.

"Let's wait until next time," I said, my head tilted, voice firm but friendly. "She's napping."

Evie was disappointed but agreed. She asked to use the bathroom.

"Upstairs next to the bedroom," I said over my shoulder, as I helped my preschooler, Beatrice, out of her heavy coat and boots. We unloaded endless scraps of glittery paper from her backpack. I worked a glop of hand sanitizer into her wrinkly palms. We talked about a snack. And we waited.

Another few minutes went by before I decided to check on Evie. Halfway up the stairs, I heard the faint sound of cooing, maybe even a song.

She was in the bedroom. With the baby.

Adrenaline. Seething anger. I took the stairs two at a time. Panting in the doorway, face composed but tense, I said, "Excuse me?" It came out as a question.

"I just wanted to see her little piggy toes," Evie said, not bothering to look at my composed but tense face. Kneeling before the infant car seat where my daughter had fallen asleep, Evie swept a fingertip over the baby's forehead, tracing bathroom germs across her pouty lip.

"Please don't wake her," I said, my voice shaking.

"I won't," she replied, steady.

"Come out of there," I stage-whisper-barked. "Now!"

Nothing.

Then: "Please?" Another question.

Evie wiggled out of a squat and sat down cross-legged on the floor, presumably to get more comfortable. She rested a hand on the baby's thigh.

"Let's go." I tried to sound commanding, but containing rage had weakened my voice. "Eviiiiie," I whisper-whined. And finally: "I hate you," but silently to myself.

It was true. I hated Evie, the three-year-old daughter of my favorite local friend. I hated this cute, articulate, and smart little girl whose stubborn will, bullying and fearless nature, and total disregard for anyone's feelings—young or old—wrecked every encounter I had ever had with her. I dreaded seeing Evie. Just thinking of her put me in a bad mood. Now here she was in my home, in my bedroom, looking at—wait, touching!—my baby. I hated her for ignoring me. I hated her for, once again, forcing me to reckon with my aversion to conflict. I hated her for making me hate. Evie made apparent my inability to shield my girls from the weakest of predators—a young child. Especially for that, I hated her.

I lowered the carrier's canopy. The baby grunted awake. Evie stood up, and I followed her back downstairs to Lisa.

Lisa was Evie's mother. I adored Lisa, just loved her. She was funny, open, smart, and often exasperated just like me. She was one of the few mothers I'd met whom I was completely at ease around. I was only a halfhearted user of the modern parenting vernacular, so when I was too tired for "I" statements or imploring my daughter to "use her words," around Lisa I wasn't embarrassed to tell Beatrice "No!" or "Quit whining." I told Lisa how I locked Beatrice out of my room to keep from coming unglued one afternoon. And how I shouted at her once so loud that I had a sore throat for two days. No gasps. No judgment. She got it. She made parenting drama feel less, well, dramatic.

Lisa and I met setting up for a rummage sale at our daughters' preschool. Pricing stacks of stained bedspreads could forge a bond even between polar opposites, but Lisa and I had much in common. We were new to a city where we were surrounded by wealth, while our own families just got by. We were blue in a state of red. Lisa liked to read. I liked to write. She had mother problems. I had father problems. Our mutual attraction was instant. Girl crush? Maybe. It was just so easy with Lisa, easy and fun. We had the makings of Oprah and Gayle, without the stylish pantsuits.

But we didn't come alone.

Behind a foldout table of rummage-sale VCRs and gently used Naturalizer slip-ons, Lisa and I pointed at our daughters through a window to the playground. Beatrice held on tight in a swing, while another girl carefully pushed her higher. Evie was dumping wet sand and dirt at the bottom of a slide, while James stood at the top crying.

"That's mine over there," Lisa said, "playing with James."

Our first playdate: Lisa's house. Things fell apart quickly—screaming, tears, yanking, pouting. Anesthetizing them in front of a *Little Bear* DVD didn't help—Evie kicked at Beatrice until she cleared the three-seater sofa facing the screen. The girls were tired, I reasoned. And it's hard to share your own space and toys. The next time, we brought new ones, two of everything. Evie took both. The rest was a repeat.

We tried again, this time outside. In the wading pool, Evie blocked Beatrice from the tiny slide. She pushed her in the water, hogged the hose, and threw grass. I tried getting Beatrice to stand up to her, at least to tell her "no," but it wasn't in her personality to fight back. In hindsight, she was probably scared.

This went on. Sure, Lisa did all the right things—time-outs, consequences, "I" statements, words. Sometimes she unraveled and let loose an old-fashioned verbal smackdown. Lisa didn't flinch the few times I barked at Evie. But that was hard for me, disciplining a friend's kid. And draining. Plus, it never changed anything. Evie didn't sweat me.

"I hated this cute, articulate, and smart little girl whose stubborn will, bullying and fearless nature, and total disregard for anyone's feelings— young or old—wrecked every encounter I had ever had with her."

Beatrice looked battle-weary after our playdates. I told her to stand up for herself and sent her back in. Again and again.

Meanwhile, I watched in horror from a safe distance in the company of Lisa. Except for the sideshow, Lisa and I were having a great time.

Then Evie pushed Beatrice through an archway at the top of a nine-foot slide. Two hands, one lower back, and a giggle: it had been a totally intentional shove. My daughter managed to grab onto a metal bar near the opening and avoided plunging head-first into the sand below. She hung on until I climbed to where I could yank her back up. I plopped her safely next to me, then turned to face Evie. I grabbed her by the shoulders, stuck my face in hers, and screamed.

The slide was no self-defense lesson for Beatrice. Just a realization in parenting for me: no more Evie. Of course, that meant there would be a lot less Lisa, too.

I didn't tell Lisa how I felt about her kid. I couldn't even admit it to myself. What kind of person who has a three-year-old can hate a three-year-old? Young kids are, frequently, awful. They don't listen. They make poor judgments. They're self-centered. Kids are not the least bit interested in my needs, my hopes, the benefit of wisdom from my experiences. Evie wasn't actually the only kid that I disliked. I could stand being around the other ones, though. I played with them, laughed with them, helped them out. I couldn't even look Evie in the eyes. The pitch of my voice changed when I spoke to her, flattening out, turning monotone. I couldn't fake it with Evie.

So, I turned down playdates. I made excuses. At some point, between my incessant napping (I was pregnant again) and her nearly full-time job (Lisa was working again), weeks went by with only phone calls. Evie now went to morning preschool, Beatrice in the afternoon. Their opposite schedules were the perfect reason to stay apart.

Just after I gave birth, my husband took a job two thousand miles away. Lisa was sad. I was, too, though my sadness was tempered by the excitement of moving to a new city. And, frankly, I was relieved there wouldn't be another endless afternoon with Evie.

Well, maybe one more. Lisa was in a bind for child care one day, shortly before we moved. She had been so good to me after the baby arrived—cooking us meals, helping with laundry, and, yes, bringing Beatrice home from preschool. Clearly, I owed her. Anyway, I wanted to help.

I figured the best thing would be to get out of the house. So, I packed up the baby and the now four-year-olds, and we went to the zoo. As we rounded the rain forest, Beatrice had to go to the bathroom. We headed to the nearest one. After she finished up, Evie decided she had to go, too. So, we waited. And waited.

"Madeline?" came her voice over the din of automatically flushing toilets and running sinks. "Can you wipe me?"

I had already yelled at Evie for running off near the wildcats and lost my patience with her when she pounded on the thick Plexiglas windows in the herpetorium. I was counting the minutes—we were down to about thirty—before we could drop her off at home. So close.

"You're a big girl, Evie," I said, voice flat. "You can do it."

"No, I can't. I want you to do it," she said.

"No, Evie. You know how."

I wasn't the only woman in the zoo bathroom with kids, but I got no sympathetic smiles. I tried waiting Evie out.

"Please?" she asked, not a minute later. "I really need you to wipe me."

I was seething again.

"Beatrice," I hissed, "wait here with the stroller." I yanked open the rusty stall door. Evie, pants around her ankles and smiling, handed me a few squares of very weak toilet paper.

Lisa and I are in touch. She is still the person I feel safest telling the dark tales of my new lows in parenting. I can't say whether we'll be friends decades from now, though. It seems impossible to sustain a real friendship for so many years without having known each other all that long before I moved away. Plus, the distance. How often will we ever see each other? There are all those miles between us. All those miles and a little something else.

lightweight bouts:
I Have Fights with My Three-Month-Old

Elisha Cooper

Why are parents so obsessed with the first time their babies do anything?

The first smile, the first step, the first word. It's exciting, yes. I get excited, too. But "firstism" borders on obsession. And it's inaccurate. So much of parenting has to do with failing. Why not remember the bad things? The first time the baby was dropped in the bath, the first time she choked on a prune. In short, why is everything supposed to be *good*? In that spirit, the first time I drowned my daughter in milk was in late September.

Zoë had never taken a bottle. We had a plan to change this. One day, my wife, Elise, went to her office on campus for the morning and left me and Zoë alone. We thought it would be easier to give Zoë a bottle when Elise's breasts were not in the vicinity. I held Zoë in my arms as I warmed the milk and talked with her softly about the fantastic thing she would soon experience. Then I sat in the rocking chair, leaned her back, and inserted the nipple. As the nipple went into Zoë's mouth, a sound came out that might be comparable to what would happen if I tried to feed her a cattle prod. This was unnerving. I moved her to another position, turned on some classical music, tried again. The cattle prod wasn't working. Our morning turned into a downward spiral of screams and spilled milk and snot. I was doing something terribly wrong, and I would have to do it again.

Round two came two days later, once Zoë and I had both recovered. Elise went to campus, leaving us alone again. I heated the milk, prepared the soothing nursing environment, and inserted the cattle prod. Zoë started bellowing immediately. Again, I changed positions, but her crying only intensified. I held her too tightly and she pooped, and I ran upstairs and changed her diaper, her legs straight and quivering. And because she was on her back, she threw up what little milk had gotten into her and gagged and started shrieking as if I were killing her, which I sort of felt like I was, or at least like I wanted to. So, I shoved a pacifier into her mouth, which only made her throw up more. I had completely lost my cool. She was furious. I was furious. She was screaming; I was screaming inside. My jaw felt like it was made of steel. Finally, I went for a walk outside, as I figured it would be more difficult for me to strangle my daughter and dispose of her body in view of the neighbors.

Parenting is not a competition I am having with Elise, but I do know that if it is one, it is one that I am losing. She's got the biological edge (who wouldn't prefer Elise's breasts?), so I know Zoë's rejection of me isn't personal. But Elise also has something essential that I do not have. She has the ability to deal with frustration, while I am a hair-trigger away from disaster. I can't shake the feeling that Zoë is onto this—that this is, in fact, personal. I think Zoë senses my frustration and feeds off it as opposed to the milk in the bottle. And what baby would respond to a father who says, "Drink the damn milk, *please!*"?

Round three, a week later. This time doesn't even involve milk—we fight just for the sake of fighting. Elise and I are at a friend's house in Oakland for dinner. Zoë starts crying, and I walk outside to, in theory, calm her. I lose my composure in an instant. It's not quite clear to me why. Even as I halfheartedly sing, let her suck my arm, point out the moon, she knows I am upset and everything I do just makes her madder. She starts hyperventilating. She's glaring right into my eyes. I'm glaring right back. It's like we're facing each other from either end of a dusty street in a Western, only instead of pistols we have similar genes.

I rarely got into fights growing up. The few I was in, I lost. In second grade, it was Casey Neil. I remember both of us grabbing the other one's nose and not letting go (I guess that one was a draw). In fourth grade, I got beaten up by a child actor whose child-actor brother played the adorable kid in *Terms of Endearment*. In high school, even though I played football, I wasn't that tough. When teammates fought, I was the guy who tried to separate everyone and then got squashed himself. In college, where I played football, too, I once lined up across from a defensive back, and when he snarled, "I'm going to fuck your mother after the game," I remember thinking, "Wait, how does he know my mother?" So, I don't think of myself as a fighter.

"But here I am in what feels like the fight of my life: a battle with a baby."

But here I am in what feels like the fight of my life: a battle with a baby. I'm fighting a thing the size of a Muppet who makes me angrier than I have *ever* been. As I walk down the street in Oakland, I am yelling (under my breath though, so as not to arouse suspicion), *Stop it! Stop crying!* And just before the urge to throw Zoë in the bushes becomes more than an urge, I think about my goats.

I had five goats on the farm in Connecticut where I grew up. When they were babies, I nursed them from a bottle. I milked them every morning once they were grown. And, every day, I took them for walks. They were well behaved, except when they didn't want to be. Sometimes, before coming back to the barn, they would stop and eat my father's apple trees. They weren't supposed to and they knew it. One goat who doesn't want to be caught is difficult to catch; catching five goats working together is impossible. And a small apple tree can be eaten quickly. So, one by one, I tackled the goats and dragged them back to the barn, hard, by their necks. I remember the sound of their hoofs scattering the dirt, and I remember how scary it felt to get so angry, how easy it was for me to turn into a brute. It was something I felt awful about then, and even now.

When I remember this, I realize that, while I may not be a fighter, I have a temper. I have the ability to snap, a terrible thing to have as a parent. I also realize that Zoë, with her grown-up features and full head of hair, is only three months old. I forget that she is not crying to spite me, that I am entirely responsible for her, that she's not a goat. That she's my *daughter*.

So, I bring Zoë back in my mind from her imaginary trip to the bushes, and bring her close into my arms, and take a deep breath, and think, *Who am I really fighting? Am I fighting my daughter or my short temper?* The answer is sad and obvious. It's me on me. I'm fighting myself and taking a pummeling.

What saved me on that street in Oakland was recognizing that, on some deep level, I am flawed (that and the prospect of jail time), knowing that the flaws I have are my own and that this girl and I will be joined together for a long, long time, for years; if I can just ride it out for the next five minutes, and for the five minutes after that, we will be okay, and we may even put down our weapons and ride happily into the Western sunset.

every look is a do:
I Let My Kids Wear Whatever Crazy Clothes They Want

Amy Spurway

This all started because I was doing things by the book—
doing what all the "experts" told me I should do. It was supposed to build my kids' confidence, their independence, and
their decision-making skills. But, lately, it's been making us
look like a pack of lunatics. I let my children dress themselves.
And it shows.

At first it was cute. When my twin daughters were three, I
didn't flinch at the thought of prancing down the street with
one child clad in rainbow tights, a fuchsia tutu, a floppy blue sun
hat, and yellow rubber boots. It was the perfect complement to
her sister's look: orange shorts layered over purple floral pants,
multicolored striped shirt beneath a shiny cartoon-cat patterned
vest, and a red fleece Elmer Fudd–ish hat perched on her head,
like the cherry on top of a very nutty sundae. People on the street

"Now, as I dart down the street with my colorfully clash-tastic kids, looking like a posse of insane clowns, I worry what other mothers think."

would smile, chuckle, and comment as our cute, kaleidoscopic spectacle paraded by. To be honest, I kinda got off on the attention. I was proud of my little girls for picking out those outlandish getups all by themselves, so I did nothing to discourage it. I may even have made suggestions from time to time. *Hey, you know what would go great with that tiger costume and those ballet slippers? The red Elmer Fudd hat!*

But, now, my daughters are almost six. They go to a nice little public school in a nice little neighborhood in our nice little city. And they stick out like a pair of kooky, sparkly, Technicolor thumbs. Which has me seriously questioning my decision to give them free rein in their closets and worrying that their clothing choices reflect badly on me. Now, as I dart down the street with my colorfully clash-tastic kids, looking like a posse of insane clowns, I worry what other mothers think. I worry that they are judging me, whispering that only an LSD-dropping social maladjust would allow her children to go out in public dressed like that. But I am not an LSD-dropping social maladjust. Haven't been for quite some time. In fact, I spent the last six years cultivating the attitude that I was a far *better* parent than those whose murmurs I'm now suddenly paranoid about: Those who forbade the public wearing of tutus with rubber boots. Those who confined their kids' clothes to classic shades of tasteful, sophisticated, and dull. Those whose children's outfits failed to inspire seizures in epileptic bystanders. *I* didn't shackle my children with the notion that clothing had to match. *I* didn't push my kids to blend in with the sheepish crowd. *I* was too busy teaching them to be creative and carefree. To be *individuals*. And I was pretty damn smug about it.

See, I'm no clotheshorse. I'm more like a clothes donkey. And ever since the thorough heckling I endured for the trendy, red crushed-velvet corset/coffin-lining/pirate-shirt hybrid I wore in grade ten, I've avoided taking risks with my wardrobe. My outfit options fall into three categories: black hanging-around-the-house clothes, black going-out-in-public clothes, and crazy-things-I-bought-on-impulse-but-don't-have-the-guts-to-actually-wear clothes. But I always wanted to be the girl who could pull off the plaid-miniskirt-over-ripped-jeans look. Maybe with a purple cashmere sweater, a stripe-y knit scarf, peacock feather earrings, and a blue fedora. So, maybe by letting my kids continue to dress like the rainbow riot squad, I've been doing a little vicarious living. And maybe it's time I stopped. Maybe I should put the tutus and wacky hats back in the dress-up trunk where they belong. Maybe I should sit my girls down and explain the importance of not wearing multicolored horizontal *and* vertical stripes with polka dots *and* jumbo floral prints. Maybe I should make some room in their closets for shades of tasteful, sophisticated, and, yes, even dull, before my unsuspecting daughters and their fashion non-sense become targets of other kids' cruelty and insecurity. But it might be too late for all that, as is evident by the conversations that ensue when I try to stage my little interventions.

> Me: *Here, sweetheart, why don't you try this sweater. It's nice and soft and . . .*
> Neen: *It's brown.*
> Me: *Yeah. Isn't it pretty?*
> Neen: *Brown is not in the rainbow.*
> Me: *That's okay. You can just try it. . . .*
> Neen: *No, I can't. Rainbows don't wear brown.*
> Me: *Okay. But it's not like you have to wear every color of the rainbow all at once, right?*
> Neen: *Yes, I do. How can people know I'm a rainbow if I don't wear all the colors?*

Then she rolls her eyes at me like I'm crazy and asks where her red hat is. And instead of seizing this teachable moment to impress upon my daughter the value of dressing like a rational little human being, I'm the one who learns a lesson: you just can't argue with a rainbow. So, I try her twin sister. She's a little less abstract. Less likely to turn this into a debate. Less prone to envisioning herself as an awe-inspiring, sky-spanning natural phenomenon.

Me: *Hey, let's just put on these jeans so we can . . .*
Roo: *No.*
Me: *But it's time for school, so let's just take off the tutu and put on some . . .*
Roo: *NO!*
Me: *But, hon, tutus are for dress-up, so it's time to take off the tutu. . . .*
Roo: *THEN I'LL JUST GO TO SCHOOL NUDIE! WITH MY BOOTS ON!*

The tutu it is, then.

As it turns out, the "expert" advice was right on the money. Letting my kids pick their own clothes has given them control over their identities, and their choices are expressions of their budding personalities. They are boisterous, wacky, unpredictable, and colorful. The seeds of independence have been planted, and my daughters' decision-making skills have flourished. They've drunk from the cup of freedom, the chalice of choice, and decided that it would make a great hat. Who am I to take that away from them because of my own ego?

Short of pinning them down and dressing them myself every day or gutting their closets and replacing their wardrobes with nice, neutral, mix-and-match collections, there's not much I can do. And I suppose there are worse things than going to school dressed like a rainbow or a rubber-booted ballerina. Like going to school nudie. But, while I'm busy rationalizing my defeat and rehearsing the humiliated smile I'll need to flash at other mothers to convince them I am not a bad parent, my husband plays the glad game. "Maybe it's for the best," he says. "You know, like in nature. How bright colors warn other animals to stay away." Because nothing screams *Don't mess with me! I'm dangerous and/or crazy!* like wearing an electric-blue faux-fur vest and pink leg warmers. Or maybe, like in nature, the vibrancy of my kids' clothes' and personalities will attract others of their own colorful kind.

in praise of c-sections: Why I Had a Scheduled Cesarean

Tova Mirvis

When I was pregnant with my third child, I accidentally wandered into a conversation in which two mothers I'd recently met were extolling the virtues of home births and water births, midwives and doulas. When the well-meaning moms asked about my birth plan, I told them I was having a scheduled C-section. Their faces conveyed self-righteous disapproval, and my mind was immediately awhirl in disclaimers: I was having the scheduled C not because I wanted the convenience, not because I was afraid of labor, not because I didn't want to miss my manicure appointment.

"My oldest son would have died if I didn't have a C-section!" I said instead.

It was unfair to pull the "my kid almost died" trump card, and if I hadn't skulked off in annoyance and then embarrassment at having reacted so defensively, I could have told them about my first pregnancy and the months of bleeding, followed by the morning at thirty-two weeks in which there was no kicking, then the hours on the monitors where the heart rate was at first fine, then shockingly not fine, which provoked the careening stretcher, the epidural that didn't have time to take effect, so instead the general anesthesia and the intubation. It was birth as highly medicalized and impersonal as critics of the C-section claim, one in which I had no voice and no control.

I also could have admitted that I've occasionally felt a twinge of loss that I'll never give birth more naturally. Having never experienced labor, I sometimes feel like a little girl eavesdropping on the grown-ups' tales of childbirth. I pore over pictures my husband took during one of my C-sections to convince myself that this was my body, my baby. When I watched a friend's video of her home birth, in water, no less, I felt as I do when watching Olympic figure skaters: as much as I would love to do that, it's never going to happen.

But that loss is nowhere near what I would have felt had all those highly interventionist, medical-establishment doctors not been exactly where I needed them. After a month in the NICU, when we were finally ready to take our son home, the resident who'd been on call the night of my C-section told us how blue our baby was. He held his fingers imperceptibly apart and told us we'd come "this close."

Those words followed me for the four years in which I worked up the courage to get pregnant again. I went back to the same OB, who warned me I would be closely monitored. But this pregnancy was so uneventful that, by my third trimester, my doctor raised the possibility of a VBAC (vaginal birth after Cesarean). I was aware of a spate of newspaper articles decrying the increased rate of C-sections and moved by a relative's joy at having a VBAC. Mostly, I was tempted by the opportunity to prove to myself that I could do it. My mother used to tell me about her paternalistic male OB who, in the days of twilight medication and fathers in the waiting room, had instructed her to "lie back, sweetheart, you don't have to do a thing," to which I'd always rolled my eyes, confident of my physical capabilities and glad for all that had changed in the world.

If I'd tried, and all had gone well, perhaps this would be an essay in praise of VBAC. But that, of course, would only be evident in hindsight, when the result of the birth was cradled in my arms. But since I had not yet crossed over to that safe other side, what my prior experience had taught me most starkly was that birth was not a process I could control. The incision scar fades after a year or two, but the scars of near-tragedy are etched more permanently, making it hard to care about the experience, rather than the result, of birth.

My scars also make it hard not to hear a tone of triumphalism on the part of some who are lucky (because, after all, that is what it is) enough to have the birth of their dreams. Or not to hear narcissism in the wishful fantasy that it is simply a matter of "trusting my body," or folly in the idea that what matters most in a birth is your own experience of it. Surely, the current obsession with the process of birth comes in response to the many years in which women were told to lie back and do nothing; yet, it reminds me of the bride fixated on the wedding, not the marriage, the bride bedecked with a breathtaking array of flowers, as if the abundant beauty can serve as a talisman against the harsher realities that lie ahead.

For me, the question of VBAC was easily decided when, at thirty-seven weeks, my doctor saw a heart rate deceleration. While this wasn't necessarily cause for alarm, she wanted to do a C-section that evening. Was this the much-maligned elective C, which I was choosing because I was distrustful of my body? Was

"... I've occasionally felt a twinge of loss that I'll never give birth more naturally."

this the voice of the medical establishment, belittling my capabilities, trampling my rights? Was this an example of a doctor rushing to surgery for fear of malpractice? What I heard was the voice of my doctor, wise, capable, and kind, who had saved the life of my first child. My desire for a certain experience, my image of who I thought I was or wanted to be, mattered least of all.

During my third pregnancy, with a different OB in a different city, there wasn't a conversation about VBAC. November 26, 8 AM, was penciled in on our calendars, though given a variety of complications, it seemed unlikely I'd go to term. But the weeks passed and the baby grew, until the date loomed before me, and I remembered more viscerally the physical pain of my previous C-sections. When I told my doctor how afraid I was, his nurse happened to repeat the same sentiment my mother once heard. "Lie back, he'll take care of everything."

Beautiful words, those were. Because a C-section is a scary thing, in which I was glad to take no active role. Even when it's planned, it doesn't necessarily go according to plan. This time, I knew the date so far in advance that I made sure to complete a major project beforehand; the night before, I packed a few days' worth of school lunches and laid out my kids' clothes. Most of all, I concentrated on not letting my mind wander to the netherworld of all that could go wrong. Yet, no matter how much I'd prepared myself, I still felt terror at being wheeled into that operating room. Despite the fact that I'd had every test and an inordinate number of sonograms, the moment my baby was lifted out was unexpectedly fraught with worry, as the neonatologist present was concerned about a possible malformation. While my baby was examined across the room, I had to wait helpless and terrified until I was told she was going to be fine.

Was it the birth of my dreams? Hardly. Do I wish it could have been different? Sure. But, compared with the result—my daughter, Liana, little sister to my sons, Eitan and Daniel—I really don't care. If I've learned anything in ten years of motherhood, it's that the ways our children are brought into the world mean very little for how they will live in the world. Nor do the intense hours in which we become mothers shape the months, years, and decades of our actually being mothers. And if the experience of childbirth is in fact a crucial process, then let it be the process of teaching us that our children will emerge in ways varied and complicated, not necessarily in times or manners of our choosing, neither made in our image nor as proof of our prowess. Let birth remind us that, with children, so little goes according to even the most well-drawn plan.

the baby between us: I'm Jealous of My Daughter—and She's Not Even Born Yet

Rachel Sherman

I worry our baby is coming between us before she is even born. She is here, in our lovemaking, in our sleep. On our last vacation, on our final night, I sit on the couch of the house we are renting and weep, imagining that this is the last time I will be alone and able to watch my husband swim in the lake outside the window with only the sound of the splash from his dive. Soon, she will come out and come between us, and we will no longer be reaching for each other's hands.

I watch my husband swim and wonder if our daughter will make me feel left out just by existing. Will she want to swim with him when I do not, like now? Will I feel more alone, watching, when there are two of them?

My fears are grounded in reality. Both my husband and I come from father/daughter families: families in which the father and the daughter have a secret, a bond, that leaves the mother out. I am guilty because I am part of it. In college, I hung a black-and-white picture of my father when he was young above my bed; for years, I thought I would never meet a man as good as my dad.

" . . . she will be her father's daughter, no matter what I do."

My father and I had jokes my mother would not understand. We both liked spicy foods. Worst of all, I sided with him, always. I made us a force.

Now that my daughter is about to be born, I think of the ways in which my mother has been left out and want to swim back through the years and wash those moments away. Somehow, I have decided this: if I can remember myself differently, as not a daddy's girl, then neither will my daughter be one.

Which is strange, since it seems that I have already decided I will be unable to separate her from myself. Which means that she will grow to punish me, because that is what I did to my mother. Which means she will be her father's daughter, no matter what I do. Because I can't change what I have done.

Meantime, while she grows, her father swims and I watch the sun set behind him. I feel her kick inside me and touch where I am sure her tiny cheeks are. I am secretly glad I cannot hear her crying yet, even though I often wish that my belly skin were see-through. *Sleep*, everyone tells me, *while you can.*

But I cannot sleep. At night, I lay awake and imagine my husband and daughter in the waves while I wait on the shore. They splash each other, then eat scallops (which I hate).

I have seen fathers and daughters all over like this. For so long, I thought that secretly my father liked me better than my mother. I was a better version: bigger, stronger, with longer hair, and none of the nagging. Of course, there was no sex, but there was a certain humor my mother could only laugh at and never join in on. My mother laughed and had sex with my father; I sparred with him, and let him kiss my forehead when he came home from work.

But, at night, I must remember the one comforting thought: in my childhood home, my parents had a door put in to close off their section of the house. The door was often closed and kept me out. I had to knock on the door to get to the study, their bathroom and bedroom, and the hall closet. They had agreed on the door and had it installed. It meant there were things I did not know about; that, sometimes, they wanted none of me.

On our final, childless vacation, I open the screen door and walk down near the water, where I lie in a hammock. I watch my husband emerge from the water. He touches my belly first, then kisses my forehead. I like when he does these things—the forehead feels like it has only to do with me.

"Why are you crying?" he asks, and I tell him.

He laughs. A silly fear. And nothing he needs to worry about. His little girl will adore him.

Sadly, it's a pattern I cannot break alone.

The idea of having a revenge-boy occurs to me. He will be mine; our girl will be my husband's. We will pair off, spar. A balance will enter our house someday.

But until then . . .

I lie in the hammock and my husband stands above me, blocking out the last bit of sun. I imagine myself a sexless lump, my daughter and husband laughing, outsmarting me. I imagine myself the way I used to think of my mother and touch my belly. My baby kicks, and I know my mother loves me more than anyone else in the world.

My husband gets into the hammock with me, and we swing and look up at the pine trees. He is still a bit wet beside me. He lifts up my shirt so we can see if our baby is kicking.

I feel thankful my daughter is not me, but I am sure she will love her father just as much. It is a new feeling, being this close. It is our final vacation and I am with child, with husband, alone.

bond rate: I Didn't Fall in Love with My Baby the First Moment—or Even the First Month

Lisa Emmerich

My mother dreamed she was floating in velvet stillness, swimming among the stars. She noticed one of the glittery specks glow a bit brighter than the others. She squinted at the star and knew it was her daughter.

"I picked you," she told me, tucking the bedsheets around my schoolgirl body.

As my mother retold her story at my wedding, I looked at my new husband and thought that someday I'd tell the same tale to our children.

But, when I pushed my first daughter into the world three years ago, she felt less like a fated bundle of starlight and more like a stranger.

The blue drape of a doctor shoved a slimy, floundering heap over my bloody bedsheets. I ripped down my hospital gown to expose my breast, an action I knew to be essential to bonding with my newborn daughter. The creature thrust her hand into my mouth. It tasted salty. I wanted to feel a thrill, tasting the flesh of my flesh.

Instead, I gagged.

"Gross," I thought, and felt a curtain of guilt fall over me.

How could that be my first reaction to my child?

An earnest reader of Dr. Sears, I had done my attachment parenting homework—reading *Goodnight Moon* to my ample belly, singing songs of welcome in English, Hebrew, and Spanish, imagining aloud the adventures I planned for the two of us.

But, when I first stared into Sasha's eyes, the flat gunmetal gray of a newborn, my plans evaporated. Horrid thoughts replaced them: *She is taking my career, my identity, my rest, my life. She doesn't even look like me. I am too young for motherhood. She won't stop screaming.*

Everybody trumpets the instantaneous mommy–baby bond. "You'll feel it the first time you see her," other mothers told me. Instead of sparks of connection, I felt an immense weight on my shoulders. I would have run in front of a stampeding herd of elephants to protect her, but my devotion stemmed from obligation.

I did what I thought I should. I snuggled her in the rocking chair and nursed her every time she rooted or fussed; I held her while I danced in front of the giant dining room mirror to lousy children's music; I toted her outside and pointed out the smooth green leaves, the vast blue sky, the boxy brown houses; I hummed beside her crib for hours every night, resting my hand on her tiny back long past when my fingers numbed. But I didn't

"Instead of sparks of connection, I felt an immense weight on my shoulders."

do these things because of some intense, otherworldly affection, I did them because I felt shackled.

At times, just a glimpse at her smooth, round cheeks covered me with elation. But that joy was chased by a nasty dose of self-doubt. Looking back, I think I was terrified. Maybe I hadn't grown up at all before then, although I'd moved across the country, held a good job, scrounged enough to buy a house. I had been counted on, but never by someone so precious and full of potential.

Toting Sasha around the neighborhood in a Bjorn, I began to look more like an experienced mother. I offered a pregnant friend tips on swaddling and gas relief and recommendations for baby massage classes. But, curled in bed with Sasha, I wondered if I'd ever be able to stop faking it.

It turns out I'm not the only one.

My friend Kate tells this story: Weeks after one of her twin boys began locking eyes and cooing at her, the other one wouldn't even look in her direction. One afternoon, she sat for ten minutes putting on her best happy mommy face, singing and joking and baby-talking him. He didn't even look at her. Then he started crying. She put him down. "You don't love me?" she hissed, cursing at him. "I do all this for you and you won't even look at me!"

That stoic infant has grown into an exceptionally squeezable toddler, who often breaks away from the action during a play-date just to lean his head on Kate's shoulder.

I didn't know Kate when Sasha was born, and other friends, who later admitted to harboring the same feelings of ambivalence, would—like me—never have revealed them at the time.

On the Internet, I read trite pieces of advice that were supposed to encourage bonding. Among them: sing, tell her you love her, read, talk constantly, breast-feed on demand, use baby signs, react swiftly to her needs. I had done all of it. The checklist exasperated me.

One article, by prenatal psychologist David B. Chamberlain, PhD, advocated the usual techniques but also advised parents to "make the quantum leap in their own minds by believing that bonding is a channel of communication that can bear all sincere and earnest messages."

I had to believe she was mine; I had to believe I was good enough to be her mother.

I finally called my mom, in tears. She was the first person to tell me that spending all day caring for a baby was not just challenging but some days awful, tedious, or nightmarish. She told me I was doing everything right and called me a wonderful mother.

"I have seen you with Sasha, and you love her," she said. "Stop worrying and believe me. Just keep doing what you're doing."

Okay.

I closed my eyes and thought of Sasha as a young mother. Her honey hair would be pulled off her face in a lopsided ponytail. She'd be swathed in a spit-up-encrusted T-shirt and bawling at me over the phone in her low, melodic voice.

I'd tell her all about it. I'd tell her it's impossible to get mothering right because we never know the results of our actions, and it's okay to feel unnerved. I'd tell her that she shouldn't beat herself up for feeling ambivalent, for wanting to get away from the baby, for wanting to work. I'd tell her that we'd rather not do a lot of the things we must do as a mother—scrubbing poop off the living room carpet, for instance, or staying up all night with a screaming child. But we wouldn't let anyone else do it for us. I'd tell her it's okay to hate those things but love your baby.

A little something in my heart stirred as I thought of Sasha all grown up.

But change didn't come swiftly.

Sasha said her first word—"duck"—very early. As she expressed her interests, we could agree on things we loved to do together, like scattering breadcrumbs at the duck pond.

Every day, I completed the tasks that added up to loving her—even when I didn't like them. I also took on a few editing jobs, joined a book club, and left her with a sitter once a week despite screams of protest.

One day, she pointed above the line of trees surrounding our house and said, "Boo sguy." She had been listening after all. We rambled around town, learning new things—she about the world, me about her. Like me, Sasha could spend hours at the library, engrossed in a new book. We toured the parks in our small town and picked a favorite playground for picnics. She developed a sense of humor, giggling if I put my shoe on my head or called a banana an apple, then copying me and laughing even harder at her own antics. My love bubbled up and swelled into something too big for a name.

> "... I rocked and rocked and rocked my new little stranger.... I just let her be herself. And, eventually, she was mine."

I felt so deeply attached to Sasha that when I learned I was pregnant with a second baby, I worried I'd lose my tight and tremendous bond with her. But the feeling passed. Experience told me the hard parts get easier, the bad things reveal themselves to be important—or even wonderful: looking back on Sasha's birth, I remember the brackish tang of her tiny, wrinkled fingers in my mouth, and I'm glad to have that memory. (Even if it was gross.)

When I didn't immediately recognize my second daughter's place in the weekday routine I'd carved for Sasha and myself, I didn't panic. I just gave it time. Sasha immediately warmed to Mimi, begging to hold her constantly, singing the baby to sleep, even sharing her toys.

So, I rocked and rocked and rocked my new little stranger. I smelled her sweet milk breath. I avoided the online bonding checklists. I just let her be herself. And, eventually, she was mine.

Now, I look into my daughters' eyes, four bands of gold ringed with ribbons of blue—so different from my own coffee brown eyes—and know for certain we were made for one another.

I tell my mom's bedtime story like this: "I noticed two perfect stars dancing together. As I reached for them, they twirled their way into my pocket, and I knew they would be my children. I picked you, and you picked me back."

"That's a good story, Mommy," Sasha said the first time I told it, sitting on a pink kid-size chair wedged between the two girls' beds.

"That's because it's true," I said.

dr. mom: I Left My Medical Practice to Stay Home with the Kids, but I'm Not Part of the So-Called "Opt-Out Revolution"

Tara Bishop, MD

Exhausted, at the end of a day spent chasing my two-year- old son around the park and nursing my three-month-old baby every two hours, I collapsed into bed. Just as I was drifting off, I heard the sound of dishes being shifted on the table. My eyes shot open and my head jerked up. "Honey, I'll do it," I called out to my husband, home from his thirteen-hour workday.

"Don't worry," he said. "I'll just stick 'em in the dishwasher and crawl into bed with you."

I should have felt grateful, but what I felt was guilt bordering on panic: I should be doing those dishes. That sinking feeling has become a common one in my new life as a doctor-turned-stay-at-home-mother on what the *New York Times* and several recent books dismissively refer to as the "mommy track."

Several months ago, I was working full-time—actually, more than full-time. I had an eighteen-month-old son and was slowly rising in the ranks of doctor-hood. I worked sixty-hour weeks, often evenings and weekends. I wasn't happy. In fact, I was miserable. I felt extremely guilty for not being home more with my son (even though he seemed happy to spend his days swinging in the park with a very loving nanny). I was stressed—constantly struggling to keep my home life afloat. But I was on a secure path to a high-flying career and had figured out ways to keep my life organized: order groceries on Tuesday to be delivered on Friday morning, work on my research project at night after everyone else had gone to sleep.

Nine months into my first year of fellowship, I unexpectedly got pregnant again. Instead of being overjoyed, I felt overwhelmed. With the pregnancy test in hand, I turned to my husband, tears blurring my vision, and asked how I could keep doing what I was doing with another baby at home.

He wrapped his arms around me and said, "You don't have to."

On that cloudy April evening, I decided to quit my job. There wasn't even a debate over who should stay home. My husband made more money than me in his finance job, loved going to work, and never felt guilty leaving our son.

I wasn't completely comfortable quitting my job, so I told people that I was "taking a break." In fact, I was embarrassed to be wasting an undergraduate degree in chemical engineering from MIT and a medical degree from Cornell. Before my son was born, I read "Opt-Out Revolution" in the *New York Times* and saw a *60 Minutes* segment about highly educated and successful women who gave up their work to be home with their kids. At the time, I vowed never to sacrifice my career.

Five years later, I found myself doing exactly that. The first few weeks at home were a series of adjustments. I went to the playground and tried to become friends with other stay-at-home moms. I beamed as my son played his miniguitar better than all the other kids in his music class. I loved that I, once again, had time to read novels.

But I was also very, very bored. I would spend hours each morning trying to get my son to sit on the potty. I would answer his endless "why?" questions. By the end of the day, I was dying to talk to anyone who could complete a sentence.

To fight the boredom, I began to apply my type A personality to motherhood. If I was going to be at home full-time, I figured, I would be the best damn stay-at-home-mom ever. I started watching *Barefoot Contessa* daily on Food Network and bought Martha Stewart's home-keeping bible. I made daily trips to buy antibiotic-free, locally raised, free-range chicken. I created a spreadsheet to compare all the Upper East Side nursery schools.

And while I'm not quite as compulsive these days, I continue to feel, every day, the weight of the brainpower I'm not using. Whenever I talk to former colleagues, I wonder if I can still read an EKG or diagnose pneumonia. I look forward to trips to the pediatrician because they give me a chance to discuss the latest research on autism and vaccinations.

Books like Leslie Bennetts's *The Feminine Mistake*, which criticizes women for staying home, fuel the flames of the so-called "Mommy Wars," but I don't see a battle between stay-at-home moms and working moms. All I see is a war we're fighting with ourselves. Before I had kids, I was great at my job. After having kids, I felt mediocre at everything: doctor, mother, and wife. I wasn't willing to be middle-of-the-road, so I made choices.

"Before I had kids, I was great at my job. After having kids, I felt mediocre at everything. . . ."

Judith Warner, in her book *Perfect Madness*, says, "'Choice' is the fetish word of our generation." We are the generation that took pride in the fact that we could break the glass ceiling or devote our lives to our children; society would accept anything. But it won't. It's very difficult to work overnight shifts when you're breast-feeding. There's always pressure to work more. So, we have to give up something. And if you're an educated woman, that usually means neglecting your kids or your career, and feeling guilty either way.

I have no doubt that I made the right decision to leave my job. But I miss being a doctor. My new plan is to go back to work when my sons are in preschool, but not on the ambitious track I was on before. With luck, I can find a more reasonably paced job. I expect that will mean retiring the fancy cookbooks, missing some of my son's music classes, and not always washing the dishes, but this level of compromise I can handle. And that's what I think about in those moments when I think I can't face another sandbox, another diaper: one day, I'll be part of the working world and still able tuck in the kids at night.

nightmare alley:
I Kind of Like It When My Kids Are Scared

Walter Kirn

Maisie was five and Charlie was barely three when we came across the carcass of an antelope while walking on our ranch in western Montana. The creature had been young, the size of a large dog, and its hind legs had been torn away by predators. Its eye sockets were empty, pecked clean by magpies, its petrified gray tongue was jutting out, and the top of its skull had been gnawed on and laid bare. I tried to hurry my children past the sight, but they wouldn't come. They edged closer to the body. They nudged its bloated belly with their feet.

"Come on. You'll give yourself nightmares," I said to Maisie.

"We don't care," she said flatly. "We love dead things."

I let my children go on probing the corpse because I'd loved dead things, too, at their age. Most kids do, and most country kids especially. My own favorite dead thing from childhood, I recalled, was a mummified baby robin I'd found one day stuck to the bottom of a fallen nest. Picking it up and carrying it home, I couldn't believe how light it was, how weightless, and how perfectly it had retained its living form. I kept it under my pillow for three days. Healthy animals couldn't be approached—they ran away, they flew up into the sky—but death had domesticated my little bird and made its mysteries accessible. "Poor thing," my mom said when she found it. "Doesn't it scare you?" I told her yes, a little bit. It scared me because it was so beautiful.

"How do you think the antelope died? Did something kill it?" Maisie asked me. She and her brother were holding sticks by then and poking them into a ragged, bloody hole in the creature's throat. Their curiosity was frank and clinical, but I knew how the night would go if I answered them honestly. They'd end up crawling into bed with me, craving reassurance for bad dreams. "I don't know," I said.

My children frowned. My job was to tell them the truth. I'd let them down. This failure made them nervous in its own way—far more, perhaps, than the true story behind the slaughter.

"It looks like a cougar kill," I finally said. "That's how cougars do it: they bite the neck, cutting the windpipe and carotid artery. Then they move to the back and strip the bowels out."

"Out where?" Charlie asked.

"Through the anus."

Maisie interpreted. "I think Dad means the butt hole." She inserted her stick and proceeded with the autopsy, digging green clods of undigested grass out of the ruptured intestines and

"I might be surrounded by rubble and dead bodies, but if my folks could just wrap me in their arms, everything would be okay somehow."

shredded stomach. She broke the clods open to reveal their centers, which were darker and wetter, more fully decomposed.

"Yuck," said Charlie. "Cool," said Maisie. "I like how the veins on the stomach are so blue."

As I'd predicted, the nightmares came on schedule: Charlie's at midnight, the whimpering, confused kind, and Maisie's at 3 AM, the full-blown shrieking kind. I had them lie down on either side of me and gave them each one arm. They slept. I didn't. By morning, though, everything was better, and after breakfast my children made me promise that we would go hunting for other dead things soon, as we've done every weekend in the two years since. Two years of rib cages scattered in the grass, tufts of fur attached to hunks of hide, and skulls in the mud. And nightmares, naturally. But nightmares they seem to hunger for, my kids, because of what comes after them: Dad's bed.

Kids like being scared, and I like them scared, I realize (within certain reasonable limits, of course). It demonstrates that they're growing up and moving away from what makes them comfortable into the realm of the challenging and confusing. It's also a reflexive show of confidence in me, their omnipotent parental protector. It's a stage that I have no desire to see end soon, although I sometimes wonder if what scares my kids is what they tell me scares them, or something subtler.

For Maisie, who's a precocious seven now, the fears that loom largest are of vast catastrophes that threaten to transform human history. I discovered a drawing recently that she must have slipped into a book some time ago, since it isn't a book that we've read in ages: *Goodnight Moon*. The drawing showed a large blue rectangle with stick-figure bodies falling from its sides, and some of the bodies had little burps of dialogue attached to their round, howling mouths by dotted lines. "I'm burning! Help!" a couple of them said, and across the top of the page was written, in oversize, solemn, misplaced block letter: *Nwe Yrok 3000 ded Setembr.*

"Is this yours?" I asked my daughter. "We should talk about it."

"It's Charlie's."

"It couldn't be. Charlie can't write like this."

"We did it together," she admitted.

"When?" I asked. "Why? Do you know what it means?" My kids were too young to remember 9/11, but maybe their Montessori teachers had mentioned it or they'd happened upon some photos in an old *Time* magazine.

"That we're glad you don't work in New York," my daughter said. "Mom says you have to take trips there sometimes, though."

Global warming scares her, too, she says, and for this I could throttle her liberal-minded teachers, because her hysterical notion is that huge floods will soon inundate the coastal cities, and summers will be too searing to go outside in. She literally fears that people will catch flame. Then there's something my father told her about the moon. He told her it was coming closer or something and that, in a few hundred years, the average day will be two weeks long. I'd never heard this crackpot theory until Maisie woke up crying late one night and explained it to me. She hugged my shoulders and wouldn't let me go for the longest time. "Grampa's all wrong on that," I said, but the prospect of Grampa being wrong on something only seemed to worry her further. "Is he going crazy?" she asked me. "Not at all, hon. He just doesn't understand science all that well."

Charlie's fears are plainer, more direct. A rattlesnake is nesting under his bed. A teacher at school has a gun that shoots "green rockets." When I explain to him that these fears aren't real (unlike Maisie's, which are inspired by the news or by ominous loose talk from tipsy grown-ups), he quickly and thoroughly calms down and doesn't seem haunted in the intervals. Maisie, though, never can be quite persuaded that Earth and its people aren't headed for dire, dark changes that are beyond my capacity to reverse. I wish it were only monsters that made her nervous, and not, as she once confided in me, "that all the water is running out."

My memories of my own youth suggest to me that even such grand, elusive cataclysms may not be what are scaring her down deep. When I was a kid, the threat was nuclear war. I had a hard time picturing it. There would be loads of smoke and toppled buildings and something called radiation poisoning that would cause the skin to burn and blister, but the crucial destruction I feared was closer to home: being trapped in my school, unable to reach my parents. I might be surrounded by rubble and dead bodies, but if my folks could just wrap me in their arms, everything would be okay somehow. Images of storms and monsters, ghosts and earthquakes, mountain lions and bears were all made tolerable by the way they drove you into a comforting embrace. But if something made that embrace impossible—terror.

I have a theory about human development. The reason that adults love horror movies and indulge their taste for grisly news stories is that they're reminded on some level of how it felt to be reassured as kids. To be spoken to in confident low voices while being served hot cups of milk tea. To be tucked underneath their blankets with a forehead kiss. After a certain age, however, no one performs those essential favors for us. We miss them. Unconsciously, we want them back. And maybe that's what really scares us when we're little: that a day is coming, inevitably, when there will be no one larger than ourselves to seek solace from when the monsters come. It's not the nightmares themselves that frighten kids, particularly as they grow older, but the prospect of losing that cozy parental bedroom, where even the worst dreams dissolve in caring touch.

baby vs. career:
To Work or Stay at Home?

Meg Wolitzer

Mothers and fathers of babies: I know from my own experience that it may sometimes seem freakish to imagine your children big, and entirely separate from you, and to thusly imagine *yourself* big (by which I mean oldish), and separate, too. Early parenthood is, among other things, a time of merging, to use therapeutic parlance. Skin meets skin, sensual pleasures abound, the family bed is the nerve center of the household. My husband and I used to lie in bed with our baby and say to each other: "One day, this baby will come swaggering into this room on his own steam." We laughed out loud at the absurdity of this fantasy, and all we could picture was a gigantic baby, like Diane Arbus's "Jewish Giant at Home with His Parents"—someone who was exceedingly tall, yet still sweet-skinned and peach-bald— hulking into the room. Truthfully, we could not really picture him changed, partly grown. We could not imagine time passing. We could not imagine a *later*.

But there was a later, of course. There was, it seemed, a ten-years later. The baby lost that baby-ness and did walk, then swaggered. And all the other babies in my midst did, too. And along with that, some of their mothers began to think about their own lives with more focus than they had in years. *What's next for me?* asked some of them, women I knew who had stopped working, or had put aside their work ambitions for a while, or who had realized, partly through the powerful experience of motherhood, that they had never been passionate about the corporate world they had once given so much of themselves to. As I watched all of this—paying attention to the period of time between when your child is born and when he or she is solidly out in the world—the idea for my novel *The Ten-Year Nap* slowly formed.

It seemed to me that in choosing to write a novel about a group of women who stop working after their children are born—and who suddenly find that ten years have passed and they're now experiencing varying degrees of ambivalence about returning to work—I understood that I was entering territory that was volatile and strange but highly familiar to many readers. Everyone I knew had had strong and sometimes strongly worded conversations about their own lives and the lives of others. Everyone had a very specific story to tell. And some of their stories *had* been told, in nonfiction books that took a stand on the issue: yes, women ought to go back to work because of the following reasons, or else: no, it was no one's business but their own, and so forth. But I had not seen these stories written about in fiction form, except in the kind of novels that perhaps had an illustration of a stork carrying a briefcase on the cover, and took a lighthearted (if mean-spirited) look at crazy stay-at-home mothers and overzealous female executives who had kids they spent absolutely no time with. Everyone in those novels would probably be slightly mocked. No one would get a fair shake.

I decided, when I was writing *The Ten-Year Nap,* that it wasn't my place here to take a stand about work or to make fun of anyone. Instead, I would try to write what I had seen, would try to distill some of the conversations I'd had with other mothers about work and money and love and passion and ambition, and put them in a novel that would take motherhood and work seriously, treating them as topics of worth. I knew it was not fashionable to write in a literary way about mothers and children. Right away, it was as though you were putting a hex sign on the cover of your novel, saying, in essence: *Men, Stay Away! Read books by Cormac McCarthy instead!* But it galled me that while both men and women would read about the lives of men, only women, it seemed, would read about the lives of women. Of course, what goes on in the home is as essential to learning about a culture as what goes on in the workplace.

For a long time, I think I had been somewhat judgmental of women who stayed at home. I went by the easy assumption that someone who worked was, by nature, more interesting than someone who didn't. But, really, I came to see both as I wrote and as I lived in the world: if you are seated at a dinner next to someone who works in marketing at Revlon, say, will you definitely have a better time than if you were seated next to someone who stays at home? Suddenly, I knew this wasn't all clear-cut,

"I went by the easy assumption that someone who worked was, by nature, more interesting than someone who didn't."

and I knew that it wasn't my place to create a hierarchy of worthiness. That's a polemicist's job, not a novelist's.

Work itself *doesn't* make you interesting, I saw, though interesting work can. My notion of "work" in this novel centers as much on the concept of "purpose" as it does on the notion of moneymaking employment. The characters in *The Ten-Year Nap* have to make decisions about whether to stay home or go back to work, and their decisions are reached through various complex processes, some financial, some about that dreaded 1970s word *fulfillment*.

These characters, in fact, have a luxury to consider these matters in a way that most women in America do not. I was very aware of this disparity, and, in certain ways, the book became a novel about class. But, even though I think the most concentrated drama about this topic takes place within a narrow band of society (and I set my novel in New York City, to heighten that focus), ideas about staying at home versus going back to work do bleed into the lives of many women in different kinds of places around the country, for whom ideas of work and motherhood remain shifting and tricky and ongoing, to some degree or another.

For me, work and motherhood have been deeply entwined. I'd been a novelist since college, when I sold my first book for $5,000 and headed out into the nebulous and small-potatoes world of being a fiction writer. I had no family money, no secret reserves of cash that would cover my rent. But, back then, in the beginning of adult life, I didn't care that I had very little money. My expenses were few. I went out in large groups of friends for cheap Indian food at night. We were all working, working, and none of us were thinking about babies. Then, in a kind of "Sunrise, Sunset" moment, time had suddenly passed, and our children were born. I watched as friends, who had had great careers or big or tedious jobs they disliked, let work deliberately fall to the side, focusing happily if sometimes anxiously on their babies and on the present moment.

And then, those big ten years passed. (Incidentally, though I called my novel *The Ten-Year Nap*, I certainly don't think most women are idle during that period. But there is, in fact, a dreamlike quality to the intense early years of mother and baby, and there is also frequently a sensation of "waking up" to the idea of something new, once your baby is no longer remotely a baby.) I wanted to write about a very important sweep of time that I had observed in the middle of life, and so the novel came out of that desire. It may seem, to the mothers and fathers of little babies who are even now pressed against you in an idyll of oneness, that none of this may ever be your own experience. It may seem—and it may even be true—that, somehow, parenthood and work and desire and ambition and money and sexual equality will all fall gently and evenly and unambivalently around you like a soft snow. I think I once thought that, too. But the novelist in me is glad it wasn't true.

my own flesh and blood: I Love Being a Stepparent, but I Love My Biological Kid Best

Rebecca Walker

In the late '90s, I co-parented my ex-girlfriend's son for six years. In 2004, I gave birth to my biological son and was shocked by how differently I felt about the two boys. I would be willing to die for my biological son, but I wasn't sure I could say the same about my nonbiological son, as much as I loved him.

In my book, *Baby Love: Choosing Motherhood after a Lifetime of Ambivalence*, I wrote about some of these feelings, and when a *New York Times* interview raised the question and I responded truthfully, the reaction was swift.

Adoptive parents wrote angrily that they would swim through a swamp filled with crocodiles for their nonbiological children. Didn't I know how wanted adopted children are? How longed for and adored? How could I be so irresponsible, so politically incorrect, so heartless as to suggest there was any difference between biological and nonbiological love?

"Our job as parents is to celebrate differences, not pretend they don't exist."

Their children were not as upset. Instead of public blog posts lambasting me for questioning their parents' love, adoptees and stepchildren sent private e-mails, requesting anonymity. Their posts were full of gratitude for raising such a taboo subject and for attempting to give voice and validity to their unresolved feelings of distance from their biological roots.

I responded to both adoptive parents and adoptees by stressing the need for dialogue about different kinds of love. I asked adoptive and stepparents to recognize that, by fighting for sameness with the biological model, they were, it could be argued, re-inscribing biological love as the ultimate standard.

I also wondered what it must feel like to be an adopted child longing for connection with one's biological parents in a family that insists their willingness to walk through crocodiles should be enough.

Our job as parents is to celebrate differences, not pretend they don't exist. Our job is not to make our children feel shame about the variety of emotions they experience. This is especially important as families find themselves navigating newer and more complex family configurations than ever before.

The fact is, the idealized step- and adoptive families in television sitcoms like *The Brady Bunch* and *Diff'rent Strokes*—shows that advocated treating all the kids the same—were never real families. The easy relationships between Mike Brady and his stepdaughters, for example, were dependent upon the erasure of Carol's first husband, the girls' biological father. Certainly Marcia, Jan, and Cindy Brady missed, or at least thought about, their biological dad.

My desire to tear down the wall of resistance to talking about different ways of loving was affirmed later on my book tour when a radio talk-show host confessed that he didn't understand the commotion.

"Psychologists have long told parents *not* to tell their kids they love them all the same," he said, during a commercial break. "Because, in fact, it is impossible to love *anyone* the same as anyone else. You love your children differently," he said, "because each child is different and has a unique relationship with each of the significant people in his or her life."

Exactly.

bumpy road:
I Hated Being Pregnant

Rebecca Barry

One day, you wake up stupid and sick. You can't remember what you were saying in your last sentence. You pour hot water through the tea strainer and down the drain without putting a cup underneath it. You want to throw up all day, but you also want to eat Campbell's chicken and dumpling soup. Vegetables make you sick. Milk makes you sick. Your husband sleeping too close to you makes you sick. "Congratulations," says your doctor. "You're six weeks pregnant." You have a thesis to finish and two classes to teach. You turn to your husband and say, "You've ruined my life."

You always thought you'd love being pregnant—that your body would take to it happily, the way it did to bourbon. But you only feel good when you are eating, which then makes you sick. "It will pass," say your mother, your doctor, your friends.

"It probably won't," says your mother-in-law. "I had my head in the toilet the whole nine months when I was pregnant. Didn't I, Tony? I only gained nine pounds, and six of them were the baby." You have already gained ten pounds. You wonder if you should go on a diet. Instead, you eat an entire pizza.

You get stupider. You can't remember your students' names, and one day you can't think of the word *voyeuristic*. You stand in front of twenty-two young writers, trying to act it out. "The desire to look into other people's lives," you say. "You know, what we all like to do as writers. What's the word I'm looking for?"

"Sad?" says a student, who will later turn in a journal with an entry that starts, *Today was my first day of writing class. The professor's boots scared me.* You consider giving that student an F.

"You lose forty IQ points when you get pregnant," says your friend Sheila, who sometimes sees ghosts. She's been calling you weekly to ask how you are, even though she gave up a baby a year before she got married. She and the baby's father, who is now her husband, weren't ready. They didn't have the money. They weren't married. She took some abortion pills, and, after they slid down her throat, she cried for two hours. Now, sometimes, when she passes a mirror, she sees a small shadow hovering near her head.

By your third month, according to the update from Baby center.com, which e-mails you every week, your baby's eyes are finally on the front of its face, and its ears are in the right place. It still has gills and is smaller than an avocado. You, however, are huge. "You might be beginning to show," Babycenter.com says. You've been showing for a month. You get mad at Babycenter. com. Also at Gwyneth Paltrow, who has the same due date as you and looks like a reed. You resent all the movie stars who are getting pregnant like they're buying a new pair of shoes. Now you can't even do this without the pressure to look like them. You are still nauseated and very pale. You tell your thesis adviser you're pregnant. "Hooray!" she says. "Have you thought of a name yet? Bucephalus is widely underused."

You want to like being pregnant more, especially since everyone is happy for you. But you feel like you have too quickly become a vessel for everyone else's happiness: your husband's, your mother's, your mother-in-law's. Jerry Falwell's. Your brother, who loves golf, sends you a card that says, "Congratulations! What a magical year you have ahead!" and this makes you feel like everything else you've done in your life doesn't matter now that you're going to be a mother. "It's not magical," you say. "It's biological. A monkey can do it." You are already tired of babies. Babies, babies, babies! The polar ice cap is melting and songbirds are dying. "Do you know what human beings do?" you say to your husband. "They kill everything. What would be magical is if I gave birth to a penguin. They're endangered." Luckily, according to Babycenter.com, Bucephalus, who has just lost his or her tail, can't hear yet. Your husband tells you not to worry, you will probably give birth to a liberal, and they will soon be endangered, too.

You notice that every time you say you don't feel good in your pregnant body, people say, "You're not fat, you're pregnant," as if being pregnant should solve everything. But you loved your pre-pregnant body, and this new one has changed into a factory that has nothing to do with you. Your legs have thickened, you've begun to blush easily, and your breasts are so busy, you wouldn't be surprised if they got up in the middle of the night and set up a cafeteria. It amazes you that no one talks about this, that the only rhetoric you hear is that pregnancy is beautiful. When you say you feel huge, people tell you you're

---

"You have already gained ten pounds. You wonder if you should go on a diet. Instead, you eat an entire pizza."

---

gorgeous. Glowing. Beautiful. But, to you, it's not beautiful. It's powerful. You have double the normal amount of blood coursing through your veins. Two hearts beat inside you. You have never felt more ferocious. When your Pilates teacher tells you not to walk alone at night, you tell her not to worry: You could walk into a war zone and say, *Bring it on. Point a gun at me. I will break you with my bare hands because I am pregnant, and you couldn't handle the nausea alone.*

You're pretty sure you used to be more conciliatory.

By the fifth month, Babycenter.com tells you that the baby has begun to drink its amniotic fluid. You assume this means that not only is it swimming around in its own toilet, it's now drinking the water. "Which means it has a dirty mouth," your husband says. "Just like its mother." Then, he falls asleep.

You stay up late reading about birth defects and the vitamins you should be taking. You are still nauseated. You look at your husband, who is sound asleep. You think about how all he had to do was have sex with you, and how you have to deal with everything—how much this is going to hurt, the breast pump, the sagging boobs when you're done nursing. You think about how much money you've spent in your life on tampons, birth control, ibuprofen, bikini waxes—about $32,560. You think about what men get away with in the world, and you can't believe they have so much political, social, and economic power.

You miss getting drunk.

One day, the baby stops kicking you. For fourteen hours, you feel nothing—no nausea, no fluttering, no slow, rolling motion in the pit of your abdomen. You are lost and unmoored, the way you felt when you put your parents on the train to the airport after they visited you in France, and their sweet, familiar faces got smaller and smaller until they were gone. But, then, there is movement again. A blip, a ripple. Unbelievably relieved, you tell your mother-in-law, who is visiting. "That's the thing about birth," she says. "You're that much closer to death."

Then, she tells you a story about the time she saw the husband of a woman who had cut a pregnant woman's stomach open and taken her baby.

Instinctively, you put your hands on your belly to cover Bucephalus's little ears, which now work, according to Baby center.com.

"That's a terrible story," you say. "That's the worst thing I've ever heard."

"I know!" says your mother-in-law happily. "She met her at Wal-Mart."

You worry that you aren't connecting to the baby. You worry that you aren't connecting to anyone else because you keep saying what you think. "I hate being pregnant," you say to a group of people you barely know (and then the whole way home you apologize to the baby: "It's not you I hate, Bucephalus, it's the pregnancy"). When one of your colleagues says the main character in a story is pathetic because she's promiscuous, you put your head in your hands and say, "Your argument is hurting my brain." "No," you tell your students, who want to know if they can e-mail you another draft of their essay, if they can make an appointment outside of your office hours, if they can make up the four classes they missed because they work in a nightclub and don't get out of bed before three in the afternoon. "That's bullshit," you say, when one of them cites a study about women abusing men more than men abuse women. You haul your pregnant self out of your chair and say, "Show me that shit-for-brains study." (Miraculously, your evaluations that quarter are the best they've ever been.) "Yes," you say when people offer you a bite of whatever they're eating. Then you take three times more than they offered you. "Go bother the dog," you say when a friend asks you how you can be pro-choice when you're growing a baby yourself, when you can't even kill a lobster and looking at a tank of them waiting to die makes you impossibly, inconsolably sad.

Then, one day, you're sitting alone on your porch with your baby inside you, and you look up at the birch tree in your front yard. It is autumn, and the leaves are so bright yellow against the white bark, against the blue sky, that you get that sharp surge of joy and sadness you always get when you see something beautiful, especially in the fall when the natural world tells us that death—like birth, like hope, like love—is an inevitable, glorious, soaring thing. "That," you say to your baby, "is what beauty feels like. You'll see when you get out.

"You'll love it here," you say, and your heart fills the way it once did when you saw your husband across the room, and you knew he was the man you would marry.

breast friends:
I Cross-Nursed with My Friend

Jennifer Baumgardner

When my son was a few months old, and my dear, dear friend Anastasia was at the end of her pregnancy, she turned to me one day and said, "I have a request."

"Anything," I said. After all, she had come over two or three times a week since my baby was born to help me as I finished a book. She'd done everything from returning phone calls to burping the baby to vacuuming. When she tipped over in the course of trying to rock my son, Skuli, she bonked her head rather than drop him, prompting me to wonder if it was fair to relegate administrative tasks and baby care to a woman who was nine months pregnant.

"I want us to nurse each other's babies," Anastasia said.

"Okay," I said, immediately.

"They'll be milk-siblings," she said excitedly.

"Yeah," I said. "Wow."

What I didn't do was yell, "OMIGOD! THAT IS SO BIZARRE THAT YOU WANT TO DO THAT!" But that was my first internal reaction. Second internal reaction: how am I going to get out of this when I already said okay?

The issue for me seemed clear. It was one of health. You can't let other babies drink your milk. Skuli certainly couldn't drink her milk. I practiced how I would explain that to her. *Anastasia, my milk is specially formulated with antibodies perfectly designed just for Skuli. . . .* But then the whole history of wet nurses popped into my head—obviously, babies can and do drink other mothers' milk.

On the Web, both the Centers for Disease Control and La Leche League discourage "cross-nursing"—both citing the possibility that either mother might have serious communicable diseases. (Many diseases, including HIV, hepatitis, and syphilis, can be transmitted by human breast milk.) But neither of us has any of those diseases. So, I called my father, who is a doctor and not a hippie, to see if there were any medical reasons not to let a healthy friend nurse your baby. "None that I can think of," he said matter-of-factly.

Oh. At that point, I had to face facts about my own relationship to health-consciousness: I didn't alter my diet or quit drinking based on being a nursing mom, and I was no poster child for hale living, existing as I do on coffee, seltzer, and candied cashews. According to La Leche League, I shouldn't even be giving my child my own tainted milk, let alone another woman's.

So, maybe the problem was more an issue of being normal, decent parents. What if we did cross-nurse and people found out? What if our children found out?! I felt deep shame at the thought of telling anyone we had done it. Surely, we would be identified as gross and perverted, the parenting equivalent of wife-swappers. Anastasia was sort of the Angelina Jolie type in my friend group, so she could possibly pull this off, but I was more Gwyneth—superficially serene, but essentially uptight. Why did Anastasia want to do this? She asked, and I was so flabbergasted, I agreed. After all, she had vacuumed my apartment.

I worried about the milk-siblings offer for a few days and then called a mutual friend, also a parent, named Amy. Amy is very logical. She'd know what to do in this situation. "My instinct is that Anastasia sees nursing each other's babies as a way for you two to bond," she told me. "You're very close, and this is an expression of that intimacy." Amy's take was so different than the hysterical rant in my head, I at once felt more relaxed. "If you don't want to do it, I think you can just acknowledge how beautiful it is that you are so close," continued Amy. "And you don't have to let her nurse Skuli to demonstrate that." Just hearing Amy frame it as bonding took the pressure off of me and, with that, some of the judgmental thoughts I'd been having about Anastasia. If anything, I thought, it's more of a limitation on my part—I should just own up to that. We *are* close. I can tell her that I'm just not comfortable with our kids being milk-siblings.

Soon after our conversation, Anastasia had her son. Her delivery didn't go at all as she'd planned. After three days of stalling labor, she had an emergency C-section and was utterly flattened by the experience. Her boyfriend, who had practiced for months to coach her through natural childbirth, didn't know what to do to help his shivering, shell-shocked partner.

"I was overcome by how fortunate I was that we were friends and could share this parenting experience."

She lay there on her side, after having her stomach and uterus stitched back up, but when her doula brought her son in and rolled him onto her breast, he latched on and began sucking hard. Just like that, she started to heal from the difficulty of the past three days. Anastasia's luck with nursing held. She could squirt milk into Lionel's mouth from several inches away, like a fountain. She could nurse standing up, talking on the phone, and while making homemade ravioli. (Meanwhile, I had to "get into position"—propping up a pillow and cupping my breast as if screwing together a pipe—for several weeks before nursing was even remotely casual.)

A few months after Lionel was born, I returned from a particularly draining two weeks on book tour with Skuli. I had lurched past the point of looking slim again after pregnancy and was scarecrow-thin, with staticky hair and a zitty complexion that bespoke red-eye flights and Starbucks dining. I sank into an armchair at her apartment, watching gratefully as she effortlessly entertained Skuli. She listened sympathetically as I told her boring tales of the book tour. Then, just as she was bringing me fresh coffee and making Skuli laugh, I was overcome by how fortunate I was that we were friends and could share this parenting experience. Lionel began crying from his room. "Hey," I said suddenly, when she returned with him, "we never did that nursing thing you mentioned back before Lionel was born."

"I know," she said.

"Maybe I'll nurse him right now," I said, feeling sort of vulnerable in the offering, as if I were actually the weird Angelina friend. "If that sounds okay to you."

"Well, I just read Lionel's horoscope, and it said he was going to get nourishment from exotic sources this week," Anastasia said. "So, that would make his horoscope true."

I took him and rearranged my shirt and bra to expose my breast. Skuli sat on the floor, not seeming to think anything weird was going on. I put Lionel on my chest, and he began sucking. The familiar tug made the milk rush in; his sucking strength and style were different than Skuli's, his little face so incredibly sweet. It felt really . . . normal. Anastasia fed Skuli, too, and because he was older and had teeth, she got her first bite.

A few months later, over drinks and a bit tipsy in that way that makes me confess everything, I revealed to another friend, Gillian, that Skuli and Lionel were milk-siblings. "You're kidding," she said.

"No," I said. "It's true."

"I'm so jealous," she said. "I was too afraid to bring that up to any of my friends."

natural born cheerleader: I Was Surprised to Have Such a Good Girl

Lisa Carver

It's a sweet and tender moment, the first time you and your kid watch a movie together, when neither of you is humoring the other. That moment came for me and my daughter a few days ago, just after her fourth birthday . . . that brief, exquisite intersection between when this strange creature who came out of my body was mine, mine, mine and when she will be hers, when she will belong to the wide, woolly world. The decision of which movie you choose just then is *dire*. For Sadie and me, it was the cheerleading flick *Bring It On*.

After watching the film, Sadie told me—her mother, the last self-proclaimed feminist in America—that she wanted to be a cheerleader. I was pleased.

You may know me as the performance artist Lisa Suckdog, who peed in a litter box, or as the publisher of the dark and disgusting zine *Rollerderby*, or as the chronicler of my real-life sexual exploits. But, once upon a time, I was small and shy and good, and I joined the cheerleading squad. I had to get up on frosty mornings, when other teens slept in, and train. I had to jump and yell and smile when I was sick. I had to support the

---

" . . . cheerleading teaches lessons of teamwork, training, and trust. It's hard."

---

football team, even—especially—when they were doing badly and everyone was against them, and us, for being on the losing side. The enthusiasm and oomph I managed to infuse into my tawdry chosen professions throughout a repressed and depressed, ironic and apathetic era (the '90s) had to have come, in part, from having been a cheerleader. Whatever weird, dirty things I did, I did them with *feeling*. And when it was cool to gaze at your shoes and mumble, I was one of the few you couldn't help but hear. Bless me, I was always loud. And I always worked hard. I didn't care who was against me. So, I take cheerleading movies very seriously.

The plot of *Bring It On* is this: Big Red, departing captain of the ultra-successful San Diego Toros cheer team (winners of the Nationals competition, five years in a row!), has just handed over the crown to nice girl Torrance (Kirsten Dunst). A little detective work reveals to Torrance that the legacy of Nationals trophies is a lie: Big Red was ripping off cheers invented by the black, better-but-unknown Compton Clovers, who were too poor to make it to Nationals (held in Florida) and show the judges what they had . . . until now.

Suddenly, everyone, it seems, has turned against Torrance: her squad, the whole school, her ditzy boyfriend (who advises her to give up captain-hood and let someone more qualified—"bitchier"—take over and "deal with the politics" in these dark times of stolen cheers discovered). Only one person believes in Torrance's ability to lead: Cliff, the unlikely antihero, a new kid in school, with black clothes, a lopsided grin, and a love of guitar chords circa 1977 to 1983. "Never mind the crap," he advises her (while pushing her on a swing . . . *sigh*). "You can do it."

Bring It On, like many cheerleading movies, deals with overcoming adversity, and the plot pivots on a question girls are too seldom asked to ask themselves: would you allow truth to triumph over glory?

That choice, posed in coming-of-age girl movies, is too often answered in this way: "Neither. I'll take option C, a husband." *Grease*, the movie my mother took me to during my window of still-formingness, also starred a cute, blonde, popular, virgin cheerleader—Sandy—who, like Torrance, had to decide between the bad-boy outsider and the cute, blond, popular, sporty, normal boy. But, while Sandy flounders in a masochistic orgy of choosing, based on who has greater need of her never-ending forgiveness (if only my mother had heard of deconstruction before allowing me to watch that movie forty-nine times during my tender years!), Torrance makes her choice based on who supports her in her dream to be the best head cheerleader she can be.

Yes, I said *leader*. Every problem and every solution in *Bring It On* is generated by a girl. Name me one other movie like that. Sure, Sigourney Weaver survives the alien predator. But she didn't *instigate* the battle between them. And, whereas the apex of competition in *Grease* is the drag race between Danny and that leering, pit-faced man, while Sandy watches supportively from the bleachers, the high stakes in *Bring It On* are Torrance and the totally hot Compton Clovers captain showing the judges and the general public what they can do, with *Cliff* watching and supporting from the bleachers. (But he's not a useless pansy. . . . Torrance does incorporate part of a punk rock song he wrote into her team's routine.)

So, while it's Torrance's ever-changing hairdos that drew Sadie in, just like Sandy's 'dos did with me—along with the sleepovers, makeovers, and best friendships—the lessons Torrance imparts once she's got my little girl by the roots are so superior to the one I got: tart yourself up and your man will change for you, and you'll fly off together (literally) in a levitating car to fulfill your dreams of having sex and being in love and . . . that's about it, no dream beyond that.

When Sadie told me her decision to become a cheerleader, too, I said, "You know that means you'll have to exercise, even when you don't feel like it, and do things for the team . . . hard, dirty work, like washing muddy cars to raise money. Are you willing?" She answered with a resolute, "Yes!"

I don't know why cheering has such a fluffy rep. In *Bring It On* and in real life, cheerleading teaches lessons of teamwork, training, and trust. It's hard. When I left that world for anarchism at sixteen, I realize now, I was trading down. At the time, it looked like insomnia, angst, and blackouts were more meaningful, but, in fact, they were the path of least resistance, leading me to have less resistance to just about anything.

Bring It On is a bit dark for a four-year-old (but so is the world, sister!). The word *ass* is used about twenty times. And Sparky, the abusive choreographer, pops pills and smashes a stool. But only because he has a dream. He *really cares* about "spirit fingers." It's good to care that much about something.

That's what I want for Sadie: that she cares, no matter what it is she chooses to care about.

the misanthrope:

I hate Maisy Mouse. *Hate.*

Shalom Auslander

My son is a seventeen-month-old Magellan, a toddling Columbus, an infant Jacques Cousteau when the lid of the toilet is accidentally left open, and he explores his strange new world with cheerful eyes, an endless curiosity, and a wonderfully optimistic, if still unsteady, stride. There are so many things I want to tell him.

I want to tell him that we love him without condition.

I want to tell him how lucky we are to have him in our lives.

And I want to tell him that Maisy is serious, serious bullshit.

"Bookie," says my son, handing me a Maisy book and climbing onto the couch. "Mayshee."

Maisy is a mouse, poorly drawn and shoddily inked by a cynical English con artist named Lucy Cousins. There are thirteen million Maisy books in print, and Lucy is, as the back cover indicates, "beloved by millions of people around the world."

People are idiots.

I want to tell him that, too.

"Dada," my son implores me. "Bookie."

"Not Maisy, buddy, please, anything but Maisy."

"Mayshee," he nods, snuggling up beside me. "Mouse."

She's playing you, man, I want to tell him. *Lucy's playing everybody. How long does this crap take her, five minutes a book? It looks like a two-year-old drew it. It sounds like a one-year-old wrote it. I honestly don't think she draws these, buddy, I've got to tell you. I think she's abducted a bunch of kids, and I think she keeps them at the bottom of a well, and every morning she passes a bucket down to them filled with markers and drawing paper.* She draws the mousy with a grin, or else she gets the hose again. *Lucy doesn't give a shit, son, trust me. She's got bills. She's got a new house in the Lake District. She's pimped out her Hummer. Those kids' parents are worried, son. I know, I'm a parent now, too. And I've seen the posters. "Have you seen Timmy?" "Have you seen Sally?" No, but I've seen their work. And it sucks. And they're in a well in England. Beloved? She should be arrested.*

In *Maisy Takes a Bath*, Maisy takes a bath. The end. Maisy, to recap, takes a bath. There's no obstacle to the bath, no journey to the bath, nothing to learn from the bath—not even a "This is a shirt and this is pants," no "Is the water too hot?" or "Is the water too cold?" I'm not looking for *The Brothers Karamazov*, but, Christ, show a little effort. Know what happens in *Maisy Makes Lemonade*? Maisy makes lemonade. Know what happens in *Maisy Goes to Bed*? Maisy goes to bed. Know what happens in *Maisy's Creator Gets Slapped*?

"Bookie," my son implores me.

"*Maisy Takes a Bath*," I read. "By Lucy Cousins."

"Mayshee," he says.

"Where's Mayshee?" I ask.

"Tub-tub," he says.

He leans over and kisses Maisy.

There are so many, many things I want to tell him.

I anticipated some difficulties, of course. That's what you do when you decide to have children—you anticipate the difficulties.

I figured time would be a big one. Our friends with children always seemed harried. "Not enough hours in the day," they said. "You'll see."

But I haven't. I have a fairly flexible work schedule and can sometimes work from home. My wife still does her thing, I still do my thing, and we still do "other things" together as often as we always have.

Money. I figured money would be an issue. The same friends that always seemed harried also always seemed broke. "Diapers aren't free, you know."

Diapers aren't free. They're nine bucks for a pack of forty. Twenty-two cents a poop. The first few years are relatively inexpensive. I'm sure money will become an issue soon, but it hasn't yet; friends bring over old toys, yard sales sell old clothes, and if we ever need some quick cash, I can always write something dirty.

Friends, social life, sex, money, time; I anticipated difficulties with all these things before our son was born. What I hadn't anticipated was his complete lack of skepticism. His wide-eyed non-pessimism. His (ugh) optimism. And optimism is a bitch.

"What a silly mouse!" I say. "She's in the tub!"

My son laughs. "May-shee! Tub-tub!"

"Look! She's splashing! Is she splashing in the tub???"

"Splasheen!"

Because I want to tell him, but I can't.

I want to tell him that the applesauce in his "Organic Baby" applesauce is the same goddamn applesauce that's in Mommy and Daddy's applesauce, only with a picture of a baby girl on the label and three times the price.

"Baby," he says when I bring out the jar. "Girl!"

He leans over and kisses her.

There are so many, many things I want to tell him.

Whore, I want to correct him. *Shill. The blonde-haired, pink-ribboned brainchild of some pathetic brand manager—"VP, Apple-sauce"—at some Allied Trans-Global Foods and Heavy Machinery Concern, Inc., "Making Good Things for Good People!"*

"Girl," says my son, pointing to the girl on the jar. "Hap-pee."

She better be, I want to tell him, *or Mother Showbiz gives her the strap. If she's lucky, she'll end up doing the weather on the Local 8 news-cast; more than likely, she'll end up doing porn. You know how many Gerber babies grow up to do porn? A lot*, I want to tell him. *Trust me.* But I can't.

I want to tell him the balloon that Doctor O'Connor gives him is not just a balloon. That it's a pharmaceutical promo-tional item. That it says *Adderall XT* on it. That the drug com-panies hope that the kids go home with the balloon, and the parents see *Ask your doctor* on it and think, *Hey, I should ask my doctor*, which sounds incredibly stupid, but, hey, thirteen million people bought *Maisy*, right?

I want to tell him, but I can't.

I want to tell him Clifford the Dog is sending the wrong message about being biggest and having the best and that the name of the character on his new bouncing ball is Dora the Explorer, a show that airs on a channel called Nickelodeon, and I bought it because there were no balls for sale in the store *without* characters from Nickelodeon on them, and that Nickelodeon is owned by Viacom, and Viacom owns the store, and I want to tell him that the Fisher-Price Stride-to-Ride sitting in the corner is a gift from my mother, who thinks she can buy her way into his life with a few plastic trinkets, and . . .

"Bookie," says my son.

Time? Not an issue. Money? No problem yet. The tough part of parenting? The really, really tough part?

"What a nice present from Grandma!"

"Can you say Dora? Daw-ruh! She's an explorer! Do you want to be an explorer?"

"What a pretty balloon! Can you say thank you to Doctor O'Connor?"

Suddenly, I'm Mr. Roarke at the opening of *Fantasy Island—* "*Smiles, everyone, smiles!*"

Tough, tough stuff.

"Bookie," says my son.

He has returned from his book box with *Old Hat New Hat*, a Berenstain Bears book that, frankly, encourages classism and neglect for the workingman under the guise of non-materialism. Sure, the bear comes to realize that his old hat was better than a new hat, but he's also wasted the poor hat-shop owner's entire business day, and there's never a thought for that poor schmuck. The man mobilizes every member of his sales staff, brings out every goddamn hat in his inventory—hell, at one point, he needs a *wheelbarrow* to bring out enough hats to satisfy this spoiled little shit—and I'm supposed to be impressed that Berenstain Junior walks out at the end of the story without buying anything? Hooray for him? Maybe, if he weren't the wealthy son of a famous children's book family, he would understand that some people have to work for a living. That you don't just get to stroll around wasting people's time because you need to learn a lesson about hats, okay? You know what? You know what? Fuck you, Berenstain, all right? Fuck all of . . .

"Hat," says my son, pointing to the book.

"Hat," I say. "That's right. Is that a shiny hat?"

"Shy-nee."

"It's a very shiny hat! What is that? Is that a bear?"

He holds up his hands like bear claws and roars. I hug him tightly and kiss his neck. He leans back against my chest and hands me another book.

"More," he says. "May-shee."

"Okay," I say. *Maisy Drives.*

He leans forward and kisses Maisy again.

"Aww," I say. "That's so nice, buddy! Is that her friend Tallulah? Can you give Tallulah a kiss?"

Tough stuff. Tough, tough stuff.

street walkers:
Why I'm Raising My Children in the City

Steven Johnson

The year before my wife and I had our first child, I wrote a book that was partially a celebration of the connected city. My inspiration was Jane Jacobs's classic, *The Death and Life of Great American Cities*, and its argument for the social benefits of teeming sidewalks and public characters and dense, mixed-use development. We were living, at the time, in the very neighborhood that Jacobs had written about so movingly forty years earlier: Manhattan's West Village. But, even as I wrote my paean to Jacobs and her sidewalk symphonies, I had an occasional pang of guilt, a sense that perhaps I was romanticizing my neighborhood. I liked walking about the streets as much as the next guy, of course, but my encounters with the strangers I stumbled across in my roaming weren't any more profound than what I remembered from prowling suburban malls as a youth. Conversations

"... children help create the kind of urban space we like to think we belong to: a space of connections, of links."

with anyone, beyond the most mundane talk of weather, were limited almost entirely to cabdrivers, and even those seemed increasingly rare.

Then our son was born, and all that began to change.

I first noticed it in our building's elevators. Our son didn't obey the golden rules of New York City elevator decorum. He didn't stare blankly at the closed doors or the floor numbers, as though he were alone in the space. He stared directly at people. Sometimes he tried to communicate with them. In our building, there were some well-trained Manhattanites, who pretended as though they weren't being stared at, who ignored the giggles and the da-da-das. But most of our neighbors cracked a smile, and a little conversation ensued. Nothing epic, of course, but enough to transmit a few particles of information: names, ages, other kids. The next time we ran across each other in the elevator or the lobby or the grocery store, they'd call out to my son, marvel at how much he'd grown. Some days, it seemed like he was on a first-name basis with half the building. And he hadn't even started talking yet.

Those connections extended all the way down the block—to the guy at the deli, the dry cleaner, the sandwich shop, even the baristas at Starbucks. I used to joke that if he ever came back as a teenager and tried to buy booze underage at the wine store down the street from us, he'd be busted immediately because the guys there know exactly when he was born (not to mention how much he weighed).

Then we had a second child and moved to Park Slope in Brooklyn, and the web of connections thickened. We've made dozens of friends through casual, kid-facilitated encounters at the playground or the local coffee shop or just sitting on our stoop eating ice cream. More often than not, the kids start the conversation, but the grown-ups end up finishing it. In the five years we lived in our apartment building in the West Village, on only one occasion did we step into one of our neighbors' apartments. In Brooklyn, we've had our neighbors over for brunch or a backyard barbecue countless times.

This isn't to imply that our kids are unusually outgoing. Any parent who lives in the city will recognize the phenomenon immediately. Children strengthen the connective tissue of urban streets. My wife and I happen to be at the age of viral parenting: every other week, it seems, another close friend of ours is having their first kid, or a second one. And not one of those couples—a dozen or so, in the extended group—is even contemplating a move to the suburbs. We're staying put partially because we're not ready to give up the city ourselves, and partially because we want our kids to be exposed to the diversity and energy of the metropolis. But I think we're staying for another reason, too, which is that we've come to recognize that children help create the kind of urban space we like to think we belong to: a space of connections, of links.

"Children help create a city where diversity is not just a slogan...."

My book had included an extended analogy between the way that ant colonies organize themselves into robust communities and the unplanned, bottom-up way that city neighborhoods form. Ants secrete pheromones as a way of communicating with other ants that they stumble across in their meanderings; out of those multiple interactions, the broader unit of the colony takes shape. As Jacobs observed more than forty years ago, something equivalent happens in successful city neighborhoods, which rely on the chance interactions of sidewalk life to create the magic of city living. Jacobs's vision was an implicit critique of the automobile-centric city, where the channels of communication were necessarily limited by the speed of highway traffic, where the only chance encounters were car accidents. Pedestrian-centric cities, on the other hand, broadened the channels linking people, making the city into a web of connections rather than a space of isolated units, each trapped in their own solitary vehicle.

But, after we moved to Brooklyn, I started to think that maybe there was something even better than the pedestrian-centric city: the stroller-centric city. Kids made the sidewalks more lively and humane spaces, but they did something else as well: they spread the pheromones more thickly; they made connections happen between strangers who otherwise wouldn't have reached out to one another. The addition of our children transformed our sidewalk promenades. Strangers suddenly had a reason to talk to us, and I had a reason to talk to them. Before long, we stopped being strangers.

The beautiful truth of urban parenting is that it flows against the current of traditional clichés about parenting in the suburbs: rather than pulling you into an ever-tighter circle of close friends and family, making you a prisoner of the rec room and the backyard, having a child in the city makes you more interwoven in the fabric of that exposed, public life. Children help create a city where diversity is not just a slogan, where encountering difference is not just a grad school seminar topic. Children make our shared spaces—our sidewalks and elevators, our stoops and Laundromats—into places where you can finally get to know your neighbors, after trading glances for all these years. They widen the net.

how to do everything wrong. bonding:
Ask Timidly If You Are "Allowed to Breast-Feed"

Jennifer Baumgardner

Conception: After psychologically disturbing visit to child-hood home, solo, for holidays, have crazy, drunken, break-up sex with ex-boyfriend. Don't use birth control.

Pregnancy: Be freelance and have the kind of "catastrophic" insurance that covers something if you are hospitalized but not sonograms, medicine, or doctor visits. Have no end of small problems for which you have to see the doctor, including thinking you are leaking amniotic fluid in seventh month. (Turns out, it's urine, which is, at first, a relief and then disturbing in its own way.) Spend a week believing you have gestational diabetes, but, later, it's discovered that it was the glass of Mountain Dew you drank just before the blood test.

Birth class: Attend with ex, who openly resents any home-work and bolts before class is over each week to get a drink at neighborhood bar. Wonder if it would be more or less embarrassing to go alone.

Labor: Wake up feeling crampy and dig out yellow Wonderbra you've never worn before; don it. Go to hospital five hours later and immediately beg for an epidural. Get an epidural that pools so that your left hip is numb but everything else is in full bloom of pain. Make mental note that you don't have pain relief, nor will you get credit for having a natural birth. Say to anyone near you, at first abashedly but with increasing volume and abandon, that you "really feel like" you have to "poop." Although all other clothing has been removed, keep yellow Wonderbra on for entire labor and delivery.

Birth partner: Ex is there but leaves during transition to make phone calls. When he comes back, he takes one look at your vagina and blanches. Ex attempts to comfort you through contractions by making out with you; stands on IV.

Delivery: Scream bloodcurdling scream until son finally comes out. Baby is immediately whisked to neonatal intensive care unit. Head to hospital room and become the only person on the floor without a baby. Feel foolish.

Bonding, Phase 1: Visit child in NICU but feel like interloper. Ask timidly if you are "allowed to breast-feed." When son finally comes home (day four), experience feeding child as akin to placing a snapping turtle on your swollen, chapped nipples. Notice son has little pimples and have flashback to terrible high school years when you had zits.

Bonding, Phase 2: Son is now covered in white and red pustules and looks not unlike Elliot Smith. When people come to see him, blurt out, "Can you believe how bad he's got baby acne?!"

"Wince as heart nearly breaks from how lucky you are."

so that they know you know it's there. Feel bad that this is the first thing you say about your child. Try to pump bottles so Baby Daddy can do 4 AM feedings but "allow" the occasional bottle of formula (okay, use formula every night).

Co-parenting: Swing between smugness that you and baby's father literally share the work and expense of child-rearing, unlike most "real" couples you know, and blind rage that you have to parent with irrational man you broke up with two years ago. Wag finger in ex's face and whisper sotto voce threats that you won't follow through on.

Bedtime: As child grows older, have him on late schedule so he'll sleep in the morning. By the time he is twelve months, his bedtime is 10 PM; by eighteen months, it's midnight. Keep this a secret from friends, relatives, and your own parents.

School: Take son to preschool the day after he turns two. Sneak out of school, sniffling, when he isn't looking because that's your strategy when you leave him with babysitters. Walk home talking on cell phone to sister about how son is in school and next thing you know you'll be taking him to college, when other line beeps in. Learn that son is hysterically crying, "desperate," as the teacher terms it, and that you are to pick him up immediately. At the pickup, start to cry when teacher asks if you even said good-bye to son before leaving.

Psyche, Part 1: Notice son winds his tresses in his fingers as he is falling asleep, plucking out many strands during each nap, creating small bald spot.

Food: Son appears to consume about a gallon of milk every day, eggs, and very little else. He asks for Tic-Tacs and cough drops as a treat, demanding in a loud, rude voice, "Need Tic-Tac! Need Tic-Tac!" Try to resist giving child Tic-Tacs or cough drops, as it seems weird, and he's crunching them and probably going to break one of his tiny teeth. Despite anorexic's diet, son is extremely tall. Sometimes he will emerge from his bedroom chewing on something, and when you inquire what, he'll say, "hair."

Psyche, Part 2: Notice son gets up from nap covered in strands of hair. Call pediatrician for advice. Pediatrician says to ignore that son is pulling out hair ritualistically, that son is soothing himself, like thumb-sucking. Ignore hair-pulling for one day, and then take to whispering intensely to son not to pull his hair; you'll give him cough drops if he'll stop pulling hair. *Please stop pulling hair.*

Love: At son's school, three weeks into the term, as you are fluffing his hair to obscure thinning areas, receive wet, mentholated kiss from balding two-year-old. Wince as heart nearly breaks from how lucky you are.

contributors

SHELLEY ABREU lives on Cape Cod with her husband, three children, and one-hundred-pound golden retriever. She writes about faith, family, and everyday life. Visit her at www.shelleyabreu.com.

PAMELA APPEA is a New York City–based freelance writer. She frequently writes about health issues and children.

SHALOM AUSLANDER is the author of the short-story collection *Beware of God* and the memoir *Foreskin's Lament*, a *New York Times* Best Book of 2007. He has written for *Esquire, GQ, The Guardian*, and the *New York Times Magazine*, and he is a regular contributor to NPR's *This American Life*. His forthcoming novel, *Leopold Against the World*, will be published by Riverhead Books.

REBECCA BARRY is the author of *Later at the Bar: A Novel in Stories*, a *New York Times* Editors' Choice and a *New York Times* Notable Book in 2007. Her fiction has appeared in publications such as *Ploughshares, One Story, Ecotone, Mid-American Review, Tin House*, and *Best New American Voices*. Her nonfiction has appeared in the *New York Times* Book Review, *Washington Post Magazine, Real Simple, Details*, the *New York Times Magazine*, and Babble.com, among other places. She's also had nonfiction in *The Best American Travel Writing* (2003) and *One Big Happy Family* (an anthology edited by Rebecca Walker). She lives in upstate New York with two small children, who she writes about on her blog, Main Street Diaries (Mainstreetdiaries.blogspot.com).

JENNIFER BAUMGARDNER's books include *Manifesta: Young Women, Feminism, and the Future; Look Both Ways;* and *Abortion and Life*. She has two sons, the first of whom figures heavily into her essays in this book in ways sure to embarrass him as soon as he learns to read. She lives in New York City, writes for magazines from *Glamour* to *The Nation*, and teaches writing at The New School.

TARA BISHOP is a physician with degrees from MIT and Cornell. Her writing has appeared in the *Annals of Internal Medicine* and *Clinical Geriatrics*. She lives in New York with her husband and two sons and is at work on a novel.

ELIZABETH BLACKWELL is a freelance magazine writer and author of *Frommer's: Chicago* guidebook. She lives in the Chicago suburbs with her husband, three children, and a vast collection of long underwear. Find out what else she's up to at Byelizabethblackwell.blogspot.com.

ERIN K. BLAKELEY is a freelance writer and author of the blog Reality Sippy Cups. Her essays about children and parenting have appeared in numerous publications, including *Parents* magazine, Babble.com, and the *Chicago Sun-Times*. She lives in New York City with her husband, two children, and more Elmo-related merchandise than any family should own.

KIM BROOKS is a graduate of the Iowa Writers' Workshop, and her fiction has appeared in *Glimmer Train, One Story, Epoch, Missouri Review*, and other journals. Her writing has also been featured on Salon.com, and she is a frequent contributor to Babble.com. She lives, teaches, and chases after her toddler in Chicago.

LISA CARVER drives a small car through a small town to a small house in a collapsed country to the east.

ELISHA COOPER is the author of *Crawling: A Father's First Year*, from which this essay is excerpted. He's also the writer and illustrator of children's books, such as *A Good Night Walk, Magic Thinks Big*, and *Beach*. He lives with his family in New York City.

LISA EMMERICH is a freelance writer, editor, and photographer. She teaches feature writing at the University of Florida in Gainesville, where she and her husband raise their two daughters.

KERI FISHER has written for *Saveur, Gastronomica, Cook's Illustrated*, and *Boston* magazine and is the author of *One Cake, One Hundred Desserts* (William Morrow, 2006). She and her sister blog about their communal household at www.whoelsewantstoliveinmyhouse.com.

ELLEN FRIEDRICHS lives in Brooklyn, where she teaches health to middle and high school students. She also teaches human sexuality at Brooklyn College and runs the GLBT Teens site for About.com. More of her writing can be found on her Web site sexEdvice.com and on the gURL.com State of Sex Education blog.

ONDINE GALSWORTH has written for Nerve.com, Babble.com, and *SoMa Review*. She lives in Hoboken, New Jersey.

VICKI GLEMBOCKI is author of the memoir *The Second Nine Months: One Woman Tells the Real Truth about Becoming a Mom*, a writer-at-large for *Philadelphia* magazine, and a columnist for *Reader's Digest*. Her work has appeared in many publications, including *Playboy*, *Women's Health*, *Parents*, *Ladies' Home Journal*, Babble.com, and *Fit Pregnancy*. She lives outside Philadelphia with her very patient husband, Thad Henninger, and their daughters, Blair and Drew.

KATIE ALLISON GRANJU is the author of the book *Attachment Parenting* and a contributor to numerous literary anthologies. She lives in Knoxville, Tennessee, with her husband and four children. You can read more of her writing at www.mamapundit.com.

TRICIA GRISSOM is published in various magazines, including Babble.com, *Fiery Foods and Barbecue*, *Sauce Magazine*, and *Missouri Life*. She has also worked as a freelance writer and photographer for the Travel Channel. She lives near St. Louis, Missouri, and teaches English at Lindenwood University and St. Charles Community College. You can find more information about her at www.TriciaGrissom.com.

KRIS MALONE GROSSMAN studied at UC Berkeley and Sarah Lawrence College. She lives in Connecticut with her husband and three boys, is done breeding, and is at work on a novel.

MADELINE HOLLER is a writer and frequent contributor to Babble.com. She also writes daily for Babble's Strollerderby blog. A native of the Midwest, she now lives in Southern California with her husband and three children, Beatrice, Frances, and Earl.

SARAH IRWIN is an at-home mom, teacher, and writer, who lives with her husband and two children near Chicago, Illinois. She writes when inspiration strikes and she has a block of uninterrupted time (neither of which occurs often enough).

STEVEN JOHNSON is the father of three boys, husband of one wife, and author of six books. He's the cofounder of the hyper-local news platform outside.in, which launched in 2006. Visit him at www.stevenberlinjohnson.com.

RONDA KAYSEN is a writer whose essays and articles have appeared in various publications, including the *New York Times* Modern Love column, the *Washington Post*, the *New York Observer*, The Huffington Post, and *Architectural Record*. She lives in Brooklyn with her husband and son.

WALTER KIRN lives in Livingston, Montana. His latest book is *Lost in the Meritocracy*, a memoir.

JENNIFER BLAISE KRAMER is a writer in Boston, where she lives with her husband, daughter, and black Lab.

AMY S. F. LUTZ's fiction, poetry, and nonfiction have appeared in dozens of literary journals and anthologies. She and her sister chronicle their adventures in communal living on their Web site, www.whoelsewantstoliveinmyhouse.com.

EMILY MENDELL writes and works from home in the Philadelphia suburbs, where she lives with her husband and two sons. She is a regular contributor to Babble.com and iParenting.com, and her essays have appeared in the *Philadelphia Inquirer* and *Chicken Soup for the Soul: A Tribute to Moms* (2008). She coauthors the daily blog www.mothersofbrothers.com.

TOVA MIRVIS is the author of two novels: *The Ladies Auxiliary* and *The Outside World*. Her third novel, *Inside Voices*, will be published next year. She lives in Newton, Massachusetts, and can be found online at www.tovamirvis.com.

NAN MOONEY is the author of three books and numerous articles about everything from horse racing to junk food to the global economic recession. She currently lives in Seattle with her son Leo, few toys, and plenty of rain.

ASRA Q. NOMANI is a former *Wall Street Journal* reporter, who gave up her day job when she had her son, Shibli, now six years old, so she wouldn't have to ask anyone for permission when she wanted to be a school volunteer. Today, she happily runs a journalism club at her son's elementary school, with students putting out a newspaper, the *Mississippi Muffins*. She teaches journalism at Georgetown University and has written for publications, including the *Washington Post*, the *Los Angeles Times*, and *Time* magazine.

HANNA OTERO was an inner-city school teacher and a movie studio lackey before stumbling into a career in educational publishing. Today, she is an editorial director and freelance writer living in New Jersey with her husband, daughter, and son.

APRIL PEVETEAUX is Babble.com's blogs editor and community manager. She lives in Brooklyn with her husband, daughter, son, and cocker spaniel.

JOANNE RENDELL is the author of *The Professors' Wives' Club* and *Crossing Washington Square* (Penguin). She lives in New York City with her family. Joanne's Bad Parenting article for Babble.com prompted a *New York Times* feature, entitled "The Anti-Schoolers." Visit her at www.joannerendell.com.

JEANNE SAGER is a writer who lives in upstate New York with her husband, daughter, a dog, and too many cats. A contributing editor at *Grand* magazine, she writes about raising her kid in her own hometown and the mom stuff she's not embarrassed to own at her blog, Inside Out (www.jeannesager.blogspot.com), and is a regular essayist on Babble.com and other parenting publications.

RACHEL SHERMAN holds an MFA in fiction from Columbia University. Her short stories have appeared in *McSweeney's*, *Open City*, *Post Road*, *Conjunctions*, *n+1*, and *StoryQuarterly*, among other publications, and in the book *Full Frontal Fiction: The Best of Nerve.com*. Her book of short stories, *The First Hurt* (Open City Books) was short-listed for the Frank O'Connor International Short Story Award and was named one of the 25 Books to Remember from 2006 by the New York Public Library.

AMY SPURWAY is a freelance writer who enjoys exploiting her family's quirks for both fun and profit. She lives in Halifax, Nova Scotia, with her husband, Matthew, and their three daughters.

MELISSA ANDERSON SWEAZY is a writer and photographer living in Memphis, but sometimes she dreams she is a chef in New Orleans or a candy-maker in Paris. Her life in pictures can be seen at Bebedreamblog.blogspot.com. Her vast and borderline-useless collection of arcane wedding trivia can be viewed at Veiledremarks.com.

DARREN TAFFINDER is a British writer. He currently lives in New York City with his wife and daughter and is working on his first novel.

REBECCA WALKER's books include the international best-seller *Black, White, and Jewish: Autobiography of a Shifting Self* and *Baby Love: Choosing Motherhood after a Lifetime of Ambivalence*. She lives in Hawaii.

MEG WOLITZER is a novelist whose books include *The Ten-Year Nap*, *The Position*, and *The Wife*. Her short fiction has appeared in *The Best American Short Stories of the Century* and *The Pushcart Prize (1999)*. She lives in New York City with her husband and sons.

acknowledgments

We'd like to thank our publishers, Rufus Griscom and Alisa Volkman; our blogs manager, April Peveteaux; our photo editor, Lauren de Luca; our designers, Mandalee Meisner and Derrick Sanskrit; and our fantastic interns. Thanks also to Ursula Cary and everyone at Chronicle Books for their hard work. Most of all, we'd like to thank all the writers we've worked with so far, both those who are in this anthology and those who aren't. You are some of the best writers today, on any topic, and it's been an honor to work with you to uncover the truth about the tough and fascinating life of the modern parent.

—*Ada Calhoun and Gwynne Watkins, The Babble Editors*